UNBRIDLED

CLASS 200 | NEW STUDIES IN RELIGION

EDITED BY Kathryn Lofton AND John Lardas Modern

Profaning Paul
by Cavan Concannon

Neuromatic; or, A Particular History of Religion and the Brain
by John Lardas Modern

Ripples of the Universe: Spirituality in Sedona, Arizona
by Susannah Crockford

Making a Mantra: Tantric Ritual and Renunciation in the Jain Path to Liberation
by Ellen Gough

The Privilege of Being Banal: Art, Secularism, and Catholicism in Paris
by Elayne Oliphant

Experiments with Power: Obeah and the Remaking of Religion in Trinidad
by J. Brent Crosson

The Lives of Objects: Material Culture, Experience, and the Real in the History of Early Christianity
by Maia Kotrosits

Make Yourselves Gods: Mormons and the Unfinished Business of American Secularism
by Peter Coviello

Hunted: Predation and Pentecostalism in Guatemala
by Kevin Lewis O'Neill

UNBRIDLED

Studying Religion in Performance

WILLIAM ROBERT

The University of Chicago Press
Chicago and London

The University of Chicago Press, Chicago 60637
The University of Chicago Press, Ltd., London

Published 2022
Printed in the United States of America

31 30 29 28 27 26 25 24 23 22 1 2 3 4 5

ISBN-13: 978-0-226-81658-6 (cloth)
ISBN-13: 978-0-226-81690-6 (paper)
ISBN-13: 978-0-226-81689-0 (e-book)
DOI: https://doi.org/10.7208/chicago/9780226816890.001.0001

Names: Robert, William, 1974–, author.
Title: Unbridled : studying religion in performance / William Robert.
Description: Chicago : University of Chicago Press, 2022. | Series: Class 200, new studies in religion |
Includes bibliographical references and index.
Identifiers: LCCN 2021019295 | ISBN 9780226816586 (cloth) | ISBN 9780226816906 (paperback) | ISBN 9780226816890 (ebook)
Subjects: LCSH: Shaffer, Peter, 1926–2016. Equus. | Drama—Religious aspects.
Classification: LCC PR6037.H23 E6376 2022 | DDC 822/.914—dc23
LC record available at https://lccn.loc.gov/2021019295

♾ This paper meets the requirements of ANSI/NISO Z39.48-1992 (Permanence of Paper).

Unbridled

or

Studying Religion's Wild Ride

or

What a Difference a Performance Makes

or

Why Me

or

Learning Onstage

or

How Not to Have Sex in a Stable

or

Doing Things with Imagination

or

Making Ways

To my students

Between the actor and the analyst, whatever the distance, whatever the differences, the boundary appears so uncertain. Always permeable. It *must* even be crossed at some point . . .

JACQUES DERRIDA

Horses horses horses horses horses horses horses horses . . .

PATTI SMITH

PLAYBILL

PROGRAM NOTES

WHAT IF I DID THINGS DIFFERENTLY?

That's my question, throughout this book. It's a question of method. It's a question, really, of methodological imagination.

This book is about imagining, and then realizing, what might be. It's a performative appeal for imagination, and for acting on it, in studying religion: by doing things differently. One of my methodological gambits is that imagination can make real differences. (That's a political gambit, too. Political change depends on imagination.)

Imagination, in terms of studying religion, means reimagination. And reimagination involves critique. Critique and (re)imagination come together. (That's another methodological gambit.) So *What if I did things differently*? comes with another, critical question: *How do we do things, and why*?

By critique, I don't mean criticism. Criticism is asserting and self-asserting. Critique is questioning and self-questioning. It ventures an analysis: a way of unsedimenting and unbinding. A critique enacts a methodological inquiry into methods.

Methods name norms and relations, made practices. They're norms and relations we, students of religion, practically reenact when we study religion. Methods mark our usual ways of acting in terms—existing terms—of norms and relations.

Our methods become our approaches, our affiliations, our allegiances. We designate them with our suffixes: the *-ians* and *-ives* and *-icals* we call ours. These adjectival suffixes often, grammatically and epistemically, precede our subjects.

When they do, our methods make our epistemologies. They power our knowledge-politics. They decide who and what count as knowledge, as knowing, as worth knowing. And they can preclude counting singularities, differences, disruptions.

What if they didn't?

What if I, in this book, didn't start with suffixes? Or with prefixed terms? *What if I did things differently*?

This book offers my response to this question. It enacts together critique and imagination. It does so performatively. This book *is* studying religion—differently. Its critical, imaginative acts are showing and telling.

These acts include us. Critique includes self-critique. It, like imagination, opens possibilities for differences. (We might be among them. Critique can change things, including us.)

Critique and imagination keep these possibilities open. They work, in this book, especially through questions. This book is full of questions. And they're real, open questions. They're ones I'm still thinking through.

These questions invite you to think with me. They invite you to respond. You play a crucial part in this book. These questions give you ways into this book, into its ways of studying religion. They stage an imaginary dialogue between us. And *us—we*—is a performative language-act, each time.

This setup might seem like a play. It might seem like a class. That's deliberate. One of my methodological moves is to intertwine performance, pedagogy, and research. In this book, they're inseparable. Each becomes a way of doing the other two. They're all ways of learning.

Another methodological move I make is to study religion by studying a play. That's a double move.

Studying a play, I'm suggesting, is a critical and imaginative way of doing what we call *studying religion*. With a play, this study moves three ways: through religious and literary and performance studies.

Studying a play is also, I'm suggesting, a critical and imaginative way of studying what we call *religion*. A play tangles together text, performance, practice, embodiment, reception. That means different kinds of interpretations, happening together. It means stretching, maybe changing, our interpretive ways. Plus studying a play involves us in playing different roles: as ourselves and others.

And I mean *a* play, in the singular. That's another methodological move: to study just one play—*Equus*, by Peter Shaffer—in this book. It turns out to be a major move. It changes my ways of studying, including what changes and what doesn't.

What doesn't change, in this book, is my subject: *Equus*. So what changes is everything else. That includes approaches, terms, theories. (Usually, studying religion works the other way around. An approach or a set of terms or a theory would stay the same, acting as a lens. Subjects studied, discretely or comparatively, would change.)

This way, *Equus* acts as a prism. A prism refracts light. With it, I can see in light a spectrum of colors. When I move the prism, I can see light's spectrum differently. As I keep moving the prism, I keep seeing multicolored differences in light. They're differences I couldn't see otherwise.

Seeing them, I can study them. A prism makes this analysis possible. It alters analytic possibilities.

Each scene in this book is a prism-turn. It looks at, and sees, things a little differently. Studying a single play, I'm able to dwell in details and differences. I'm able to ask questions and explore possibilities. My analysis isn't rushed, or truncated, or instrumentalized. I can keep turning the prism.

Doing so poses an analytic testing: of limits. It tests my analytic limits. It tests limits of methods I use. It can test limits of studying religion.

These limits include terms. In this book, I don't start with a set of critical terms for studying religion and then fit, or force-fit, *Equus* into them. Doing so would predelimit and predetermine my ways of analysis. And it would miss too many of *Equus*'s differences, especially ones that trouble terms and methods.

So I take my analytic cues from *Equus*. It's a play about testing limits, of norms and relations.

Following these cues, I develop a different set of critical terms for studying religion in this case. (That's another methodological move.) These terms manifest critical reimagination. They test, and push on, and push through analytic limits, to open other ways of studying religion.

I'm not sure *reading* best describes this mode of analysis. *Reading* feels too one-way, too linear, too restricted. Plus it feels too scriptocentric. It feels too unequipped to address performance's imaginal, affective, embodied, effective senses. One of my methodological moves is to attend to performance's complexities, to explore differences they might make for studying religion.

Relating feels better than *reading*. It gets at the multivalent, multidirectional, extended, immersive, interactive qualities of my acts: of thinking with and through *Equus*. And *relating* involves different senses of temporality, attention, investment. It signals a different kind of care. It's more personal.

I've made this book more personal by intensifying its focus. *Equus* is the only text I quote in my text (until the Encore). In this book, it's just *Equus* and me and you. We're in it together. And we're not depending on others for support or security. That feels scary, like a tightrope walk without a net.

It also feels worth doing. (Doing it reentangles research, pedagogy, and performance.) I want to avoid exclusions, and academic entrance fees, that citations can impose. I want to open access to this book. I want amateur and professional students of religion to be able to engage this book. I've written it hoping to make that possible.

Making these methodological moves, I'm tempted to say that this book stages a methodological intervention for studying religion.

This temptation, I know, comes from our knowledge-politics. They can be fierce. They usually play out as zero-sum power games. In these games, for my work to count, someone else's work must dis-count.

So positions become oppositions. Interactions become confrontations. Sometimes they're passive-aggressive. Sometimes they're aggressive-aggressive.

We've naturalized and normalized these patterns. We've so naturalized and normalized them that not reenacting them, especially in these program notes, is difficult. These patterns are what make "methodological intervention" tempting.

I'm resisting this temptation. I don't want to play into knowledge-politics-as-usual and their implicit salvific complex.

So I won't call this book a methodological intervention.

I'm not asking the study of religion to go to rehab.

And I'm not acting with normalizing force.

In this book, I'm not declaring or demonstrating the new normal for studying religion. I'm not showing and telling you how *to* study religion. I'm showing and telling you how *we*, students and I, study religion.

I want to supplement, not supplant. I want to pluralize possibilities of studying religion: of doing things differently.

Pluralizing possibilities and doing things differently feel particularly pressing. Knowledge-politics are pressing on body-politics.

I write to you amid pandemics. COVID-19 and racisms rampage. These public health crises, especially together, ravage peoples. Death counts are daily news. (But not all deaths get counted.)

These pandemics expose *us*. They expose precarities, vulnerabilities, unhealthinesses of *us*. They make *us* a problem.

Nothing is normal now. Old norms are unsustainable. New norms are unstable. What will normal mean tomorrow? No one knows.

This book isn't about pandemics. But it's about crises that come when norms break down. (That's one way of making sense of *Equus*.) It's about reckoning with these norms' effects. And it's about reimagining possibilities of norms and relations.

The crises this book engages are of what we call humanities. They're institutional, interdisciplinary, interpersonal, even interspecies crises of norms and relations. That makes them methodological crises, too.

But what if methods meant possibilities, not precedents? What if we, who study humanities, critically reimagined methods as openings: for other normals, for different relations?

What if we did things differently?

CAST

PETER SHAFFER: a queer, deceased playwright who wrote *Equus*

ALAN STRANG: an undereducated teenager, Dora and Frank's son, who becomes passionately and painfully devoted to horses (especially one horse) and to a horse-divinity he invents

DORA STRANG: a former schoolteacher, Frank's wife and Alan's mother, a devoted Christian who reads Alan the Bible and other stories

FRANK STRANG: a printer, a socialist, an atheist, Dora's husband and Alan's father, who spends his evenings at a pornography theatre

JILL MASON: a young woman who works at a stable, who almost has sex with Alan there, and who has a nervous breakdown afterward

HARRY DALTON: a stable owner who employs Jill and (later) Alan

NUGGET: a chestnut horse who becomes intimately involved with Alan, romantically and ritually

EQUUS: a jealous, watchful horse-divinity who inhabits horses' bodies, whom Alan invents and makes the core of an invented religion

THE NORMAL: a double-edged divinity who sustains "healthy" norms and who demands that priests sacrifice abnormalities

HESTHER SALOMON: a local magistrate, a Normal devotee, Dysart's confidante, who sees Alan's pain and persuades Dysart to treat it

MARTIN DYSART: a middle-aging child psychiatrist, a priest of the Normal, who suffers professional menopause and a sexless marriage, who spends his evenings reading about ancient Greece

WILLIAM ROBERT: a queer, middle-aging professor who wrote this book

PROLOGUE

YOU'VE MADE YOUR WAY HERE. You're here for a performance.

You enter the performance-space. You take the program you're handed.

You take in the situation, the scene. You notice the lighting, the sounds, the seating, the stage. You notice how you feel: how this setting makes you feel.

You notice others. They've made their ways here, too.

You find your seat. Or you find the specified place for your wheelchair. You notice how comfortable, or uncomfortable, you are. You notice how well, or poorly, you can see the stage. You notice your neighbors. You flip through the program.

You're here. You're seated. You're ready. The performance is about to begin.

You know what you're about to experience (see, hear, think, feel). And you don't know what you're about to experience.

That's how a performance works. It entangles anticipation and astonishment. It mixes preparation and improvisation. Even a scripted, rehearsed performance can surprise, even its performers.

A performance sur-prises. It overtakes us. It realizes a performance's promise: to be an event.

An event is something that happens, unprevised. It's unanticipatable. An event happens, to us. It befalls us. It comes as a real surprise.

An event interrupts our senses of possibility. This singular interruption remains. It's never fully settled. It's never really resolved. An event is an opening, without closure.

A performance is an event. It happens to us, performers and watchers. A performance affects us. It leaves us affected.

We leave it affected. We leave a performance different—even if just a little, just for a little while. A performance makes differences.

This book is about performance. It's about differences performance might make for studying religion. It's about how we might perform studying religion differently.

And this book is a performance. It might be the performance you're here for.

Let's find out.

ACT 1

1.
I
MISE-EN-SCÈNE

I'VE MADE MY WAYS HERE, TOO.

I've taken more ways than one. I've come by way of a play, and a class, and a desire.

The play is *Equus*, by Peter Shaffer.[1]

The class is Introduction to the Study of Religion.

The desire is to do things differently.

That's how I've made my ways into this scene.

Scenes make, and make up, this book. It's a book of scenes, made into acts.

These acts are entangling. They entangle research, pedagogy, performance. And they entangle us. You and I are in this scene. We're involved.

I'm nervous, in this opening scene. But I'm here to act. I start with a question. It's my opening line.

How might we study religion?

I've lived with this question. I've struggled with it. Maybe you have, too.

It's a critical question of method. It asks us to query what we call religion, and how we study it. This question asks us to imagine how these things might be different. It invites us to devise different ways, and then take them. They would make different ways for studying religion: researching and teaching: learning.

Different ways would open things, like disciplines, and protocols, and praxes.[2] They would keep these things open, and in question.

How might we study religion?

A few years ago, I reimagined my Intro.[3] I started over, with this question.[4]

That's where this book started. It's why Intro, and students, and pedagogy are parts of this book's mise-en-scène.[5] This book is unimaginable without them.

As I write, I feel my responsibility to Intro and its students. That makes writing this book tricky. It's personal. Learning always is.

I've asked my question. Now I need to respond.

This book *is* my response, enacted in writing. I'm performing my ways of responding. (There are other ways. Maybe you would take one of them.)

We might study religion by studying problems, without easy solutions.

We might study religion by trekking into unmapped territory.

We might study religion by crossing lines: of what usually counts, or gets counted, as studying religion.

We might study religion experimentally. We might try things, see how they work, try other things.

We might study religion performatively. We might learn by doing. Our pedagogical praxis might be researching.

We might study religion by studying a play—in our case, *Equus*. We might study *Equus* as a case, as a way of studying religion.

We do in Intro, and in this book. This book studies *Equus*, to study religion.

Equus is an extraordinary play.[6] It's carefully crafted. *Equus* is taut.[7] It's sharp. It's riveting. And it's complicating.

Equus turns on a violent act. One night, Alan Strang blinds six horses. Alan's act sends him to court, then to a psychiatric hospital. Magistrate Hesther Salomon persuades psychiatrist Martin Dysart to treat Alan.

Equus tracks this treatment. It tracks this treatment's effects on *Equus*'s players. They include Alan and his parents, Dora and Frank Strang. They include Alan's boss, Harry Dalton, and Alan's friend, Jill Mason. They include Alan's favorite horse, Nugget, and Alan's horse-divinity, Equus. And they include Alan's doctor, Dysart.

Equus enacts Dysart's account of this treatment, to discover why Alan blinded the horses. It shows and tells what Dysart, and Alan, and others discover. It plays out what they desire, what they decide, what they do. *Equus* exposes raveling relations that become unraveling relations for *Equus*'s players.

Equus is so much more than my short summary. It overflows: with layered allusions, concentrated language, dynamic scenes, dazzling effects.[8] It's overfull of divinities, devotions, desires, deceptions and self-deceptions, relations, revelations, complications. *Equus* explodes, with what we call religion.

As in Intro, you really have to read this play we're studying.

(We'll plunge into *Equus* soon. First, we'll take a few scenes to make our ways in.)

Few students of religion study religion by studying plays. Very few study religion by studying this play. There's almost no disciplinary archive I can cite for support. Other disciplinary archives go only so far. (This book is, as far as I know, the first devoted to *Equus* in any discipline.)

So I'm not tethered to traditions. I can't secure myself by latching to them. I'm unfixed, and feeling it. I can feel my vulnerability.

And I'm not stringing safety nets. I'm not swaddling a play in citations. I'm not reducing a play to a text, or to a set of ideas. I've done these things before. For me, I think now, they're missteps.

In this book, performance counts.

That includes my writing, and my endnoting.

I write mostly short sentences. I like short sentences. They don't exhaust or overwhelm. They're not mastering. Short sentences leave room: for inflections, for implications, for readers—for you. Plus they're sentences I might say. They're sentences I might say in Intro.

I use endnotes like handouts in Intro. They're resources. They're there, if you want to use them.

My endnotes include supplementary materials that inform this study. They form a kind of counter-text. My endnotes name interlocutors and trace genealogies. And they mark possible ways not taken. (They're other ways of learning.) But my endnotes are selective, not comprehensive.[9]

Maybe you're reading the endnotes. Maybe you're not. This book works both ways.

And you didn't make your way here for endnotes. You're here—we're here—for a performance.

1.

2

IMAGINATION

HOW MIGHT WE STUDY RELIGION?

It's an imaginative question. Responding calls for imagining.

What if . . . ?

Imagination pushes on limits of what is. It pushes past them, to what might be. *Being* becomes *maybeing*. That makes ways for differences. *What if . . .* ? asks, already, *What if things were different*?

That's imagination's question.[1] It's a question an aesthetic, and a politic, and a religion ask. It ties them together, with imagination.

An aesthetic is a way of sensing and making sense. It interweaves what's sensible: what we sense, what makes sense to us, what makes sense to do. Sense interweaves a phenomenology, an epistemology, and an ethic.

And sense asks questions of value and imagination. An aesthetic is a way of valuing our senses, and our ways of making them. It's also a way of imagining other senses, and other ways of making sense.[2]

These ways are how we make, unmake, remake senses. They're how we alter, in our realities, what counts as common sense, and what counts as nonsense.[3] They're ways we remake *us*, too.

So are politics. A politic reconfigures common senses.[4] It opens different ways of relating: of living together. Political change begins by asking, *What if things were different*? A politic situates imagination's question: *What if things were different for us, for others*?

This question is also a religion's. A religion also imagines and reimagines senses and relations and us. Whatever else a religion might be, it's a way of making and remaking us. A religion tangles and untangles relations among us. They're ways we connect and disconnect.[5]

A religion, like an aesthetic or a politic, is a way of deciding, and enacting, how we count. It counts, decides, enacts *us*. A religion, like an aesthetic or a politic, does these things with our senses and our values and our relations. And it can redo these things differently.

A religion, an aesthetic, or a politic is a way of valuing our ways of valuing. That makes it—them, together—a critical praxis. (A praxis alloys theory and practice. They affect, and effect, each other. Neither is primary.)

More imaginative questions open for us.

How might we make sense?

How might we value?

Who might we be?

These questions are ones a religion, or an aesthetic, or a politic puts in play. We ask, and keep asking, these questions in Intro. Sometimes we start asking them on our first day of class.

With these questions come others.

What if we figure religion differently?

What if we study religion differently?

What if we study a play as a way of studying religion?

This last question reimaginatively doubles.

This question asks us about studying a play as *a way* of studying religion. There are other ways. Each way might involve different methods, and take different paths.

This question also asks us about studying a play as a way of *studying religion*. That's critical. And it's intervening. Studying a play might make a way of reimagining religion and ways of studying it.

This question doubles possibilities of aesthetic inquiry.[6] Aesthetic inquiry poses and pursues imagination's question. It enables us to track differences aesthetics make, and how they matter.

1.3

LITERATURE

STUDYING A PLAY, WE TURN to literature. And we re-turn to imagination.

What we call literature is an opening: of imaginative possibilities. It opens, and reopens, ways we might imagine.[1] Literature is unlimiting. It unlimits possibilities of presenting anything imaginable.[2]

Literature re-asks imagination's question.

What if things were different?

And literature responds. Literature *is* a response.

(What we call literature is, or has, no essence.[3] It's not an intrinsic quality or a closed container. Literature resists closure or enclosure. It resists being institutionalized.[4])

To imagination's question, literature responds poietically and performatively.[5] Literature enacts imaginabilities. It enacts different senses and ways of making sense. It enacts different values and ways of valuing. Literature enacts different ways of living, with others.[6]

These enactions entangle aesthetics, ethics, ontologies. They imagine, and reimagine, realities: with other senses, and other values, and others.[7]

Religion does, too. Whatever else a religion does, it imagines and reimagines realities. Whatever a religion does comes from its imaginations.

That doesn't make religion imaginary. Religion is real. It makes real differences. So does literature. They make real differences because imagination makes real differences.

Literature and religion need imagination. They live on imagining. They realize differences by reenacting, and responding to, *what if things were different?* Their (re)imagined realities might affect ours. And ours might affect others, and others'.

Studying literature and religion together, we show and tell their relations.[8] And we reiterate, performatively, that aesthetic inquiry opens critical ways of studying religion. Aesthetic inquiry is as critical as other ways of inquiry. It might even be more critical.[9]

Studying *Equus* makes ways we can study literature and religion, together, in a play. A play is a particular kind of literature. We can't read a play like we read other texts. A play does things differently. (That's one reason to study a play.)

A play involves performance. That involves us. A play implicates us. It won't be held at a safe distance. A play is interactive. It calls us to act. We play-act two roles: as ourselves and as others.

Performance changes things. And it reminds us that a religion is a performance, by bodies, in effecting ways. That poses more questions, for us.

What differences might performance make for studying religion?

How might studying performance and religion together make differences?

We'll leave these questions open, for now.

1.4

PERFORMANCE

WHAT WE CALL PERFORMANCE VARIES. It veers. It moves, in different ways. And what we call performance depends on us. It depends on how we (decide to) count.

How might we count what we call performance? As a process? A praxis? A production? A transmission? A transformation? An intervention?[1]

What acts and their differences might we count in performance?[2]

We might count formal, informal, theatrical, quotidian, scripted, and/or improvised acts.[3] A performance might be embodied, disembodied, gestural, verbal, virtual, material, artistic, activistic, private, and/or public.

These lists, I know, involve contradictions. A performance might, too. It might be and do more than one thing, in more than one way, at once.[4] And it might be and do them repeatably or unrepeatably, ephemerally or enduringly.

How we count these acts and differences would make different senses of performance. That makes performance—varying, veering—difficult to capture. What we call performance opens questions.

I can't finally answer these questions. My senses of performance are partial. They're based on decisions I've made. Your senses of performance might differ. Performance affects us, and *us*, differently. It does things—differently.

Performance names different ways of doing. A performance is a doing. It does things. Its doing does things. That makes a performance performative. Performance and performativity come together, enmeshed, in contexted situations.[5]

Performance names different ways of imagining. A performance enacts a response to imagination's question: *What if things were different*? It makes ways of imagining, or reimagining, realities. They might be ours, or others'.

These realities might be more livable. They might have and make different senses. That might incite us to act on our imaginations: to make differences.[6]

Performance names different ways of knowing. So it also names different ways of learning. Knowing follows learning. Epistemologies rely on pedagogies.

Let's turn to a pedagogical scene in *Equus*: when Jill teaches Alan how to groom Nugget. (Nugget is Jill's favorite horse.)

Jill picks up a currycomb. She begins to groom Nugget. "You always groom," Jill shows and tells Alan, "from the ears downward": "down towards the tail and right through the coat" (§16/53). "Push it [the currycomb]," Jill shows and tells Alan, "right through the coat: like this" (§16/53).

Jill's pedagogy is performative. She teaches by doing. And her doing teaches. Alan learns by watching, then by doing, while Jill watches. Then Jill leaves.

It's Alan's first time alone with a horse. Alan touches Nugget. He moves his hand over Nugget's neck and back. Then Alan smells his hand, with his eyes closed.

Close your eyes. Imagine this scene in performance.

How might Alan's and Nugget's bodies be positioned? How close might they be?

Where might Alan's hand move? Along an imaginary, extended equine-body? Along Nugget's (the-actor-playing-Nugget's) physical body? Might Alan follow Jill's lesson that "the harder you do it, the more the horse loves it" (§16/53)?

How long might this scene last?

Alan learns a lot in this scene. He learns who Jill's favorite horse is. He learns how to groom a horse. He learns how grooming feels, and how it makes him feel. He learns how it feels to be alone with a horse, touching. And he learns he wants to feel this way again. (Alan performs this learning in the scene opening each of *Equus*'s acts.)

How might this scene be performatively teaching us?

What might we learn from this scene by imagining its performance?

This grooming scene interleaves performance and pedagogy, knowing and learning. Different ways of learning might open ways of knowing differently.[7] They would be situated, situating ways. *Knowing that* would depend on *knowing who*, and *knowing how*, and *knowing when and where*.

That would remake what we count as knowing: as performance-knowing. It would mean involving knowers and ways of knowing in what we count as knowing. These involvements would mean acknowledging knowers' and knowledges' precarities.

Performance names different ways of studying.[8] A performance opens questions. It offers responses. It opens more questions. It draws us in to them.

These ways are researching. They're ways of learning, through a performance. We follow their leads.

We follow them across lines. We cross lines of disciplined protocols, prepackaged methods, preset subjects. We let ways of performance morph our ways of inquiry. We don't start assuming.[9] We start questioning.

Performance names these different ways of acting (doing, imagining, knowing, studying). It knots them together, in a praxis—for now. A performance-praxis ties a slipknot. It's a fine knot for now. But it doesn't finally fix things. With one pull, a slipknot comes undone.

That can make things messy. A performance does. It messes up fixities. It messes with things as they are.

That's what we're doing, in this performance.

1.5

CASE

WE'RE STUDYING *EQUUS* as a case. By *case*, I don't mean *case-study*. They're different.

A case-study reduces a case, to a case *of* ______. For a case-study, the *of* ______ is more important than the case.[1] And the *of* ______ risks reification, into a *thing itself*. It risks transcendence.

Of ______ contains things. It keeps a case-study contained.[2] (A case-study has to be.) *Of* ______ values containers over contents. It values categories over complexities.

Of ______ manages a case's singularity. It bulldozes case-specifics: variations, variegations, eccentricities. *Of* ______ paves over differentiations—and decisions. It overlays our decisions about what might fill in the blank.[3]

Rendered a case-study, *Equus* might become a case *of* what we've already decided to call religion. A case-study is a way of fitting: in the frame.[4] Framing *Equus* as a case-study would use prefab senses of religion to contain *Equus*, make *Equus* fit.

A case is different. A case is a problem. It's an event-made-problem.[5]

A case problematizes. It troubles. It questions. A case tests.

A case is a test-case. It tests us. It tests our ways of working. It tests our limits. A test-case is a limit-case. It pushes on our limits.

A case can disorder things. It can disturb things.[6] Then things can shift. They can open. They might stay open. Things might fall out of line, or cross lines, or move lines.

We might, too. A case might change things—like who we are, how we work, how we sense and make sense. We might imagine other ways, and then take them.

A case requires more ways than one. We have to make multiple approaches. We have to mix methods. Working a case, we follow its lead. We do what *this* case calls for.

Still, a case remains, singularly, in question. We can't solve or resolve a case. A case's problems and tests persist.

Equus's do. *Equus*, as a case, disturbs our senses of religion. It troubles our ways of studying religion. *Equus* makes us question them, because it doesn't fit in them. *Equus* is a problem they can't contain or solve.

Really, *Equus* is problems for studying religion. Our well-worn ways of problem-solving won't work for *Equus*. *Equus* poses test-questions that remain open, across realities: its, and ours, and their relations. Here are some.

How might *Equus* make sense, in its realities? How might *Equus* make sense to us, in our realities? How might we make sense of *Equus*, across realities?

And how might we make sense of *Equus*'s ending? That's a critical question in this case.

It opens another sense of case. *Case* might mean "mystery."

Equus enacts two main mysteries. One mystery is narrative. One mystery is interpretive. Both keep us in suspense.

The narrative mystery is an odd one: a whydunnit.[7] In *Equus*, we know who did what. Alan blinded six horses. We don't know why—until the end. This not-knowing is at *Equus*'s heart.

In this narrative case, Dysart acts as detective. (We do, too. It's one way *Equus* engages us.) And Dysart solves this mystery. By *Equus*'s end, we know why Alan blinded six horses. *Equus*'s narrative, through Dysart, shows and tells us why.[8]

The interpretive case is more mysterious. It's about Dysart's—*Equus*'s—last lines: "There is now, in my mouth, this sharp chain. And it never comes out" (§35/110).

What might these lines mean? How might we make sense of them interpretively? ("This sharp chain": What might that refer to? And why doesn't it ever come out?)

How might we make sense of these lines performatively? Because *Equus* is a play, interpretation involves performance. So how might these lines look, sound, feel to us in a performance? (How might Dysart say them? To whom? Looking where? Who might Dysart have to become, or have become, to perform these lines?)

This interpretive-performative mystery matters. I think it *really* matters. How we respond to these questions directs how we make sense of *Equus*. Our senses of *Equus* hinge on our senses of its last lines. And these senses direct how we study *Equus*, this case.

This last-lines mystery endures after *Equus*'s end. Each time we encounter *Equus*, we reencounter this mystery. *Equus* doesn't solve it for us.

So it's up to us. We're the detectives working this case. That's one role we play in this casebook. (Keep this mystery, of these last lines, in mind. We'll return to it.)

1.6

TERMS

WE CAN WORK WITH TERMS. Terms give us ways of working *Equus*'s case.

Terms are positional. They're situational. And they're situated, in contexts and relations, with other terms. We use different terms in different situations—different cases. Different cases call for different terms.

Terms are partial.[1] No term can account for a case. We always need more terms than one.[2] And we could always use more terms.

Terms are pliable. That's crucial. No term perfectly fits a case. Terms involve incongruities.[3]

Terms are plural. They can mean multiply. And they can mean collaboratively. Terms can play well with others, to make meanings. Terms can also become permeable, in relations with other terms.

Terms are political. With terms, we're forced to deliberate, negotiate, decide. Terms demand decisions from us. And our decisions have consequences. They make differences.

Terms are problematic. Or they can be. That's part of what makes them critical.[4] They can pose questions.

Terms are popular. They fill disciplinary guidebooks. They're often how guidebooks, and disciplines, are arranged.[5]

Terms are practical. They work in practice: *in this case*.

Terms are pedagogical. They function in different pedagogical scenes. We learn by using them. (Terms are our primary tools in Intro.)[6]

Terms are performative. They entangle. Terms entangle performance and pedagogy and research, as ways of studying religion. They entangle us, too.

This book performs these entanglements.

Our entanglements locate us. Maybe they locate us in classrooms, or offices, or libraries, or archives, or field sites, or other places. Maybe—*maybe*—they locate us in theatres. These locations might be closer than we think.

Let's try something.

Go back and reread the prologue. Substitute some words: *pedagogical-space* for *performance-space*, *syllabus* for *program*, *blackboard* for *stage*, *course* for *performance* . . . You get the idea. I might be describing the first day of a class. Maybe it's your class, or mine.

Reread the prologue again. Substitute some other words and phrases: *scholarly-space* for *performance-space*, "books you've collected" for "program you're handed," *research* for *performance* . . . I might be describing a day of researching or writing in a library. Maybe it's the library where I wrote this sentence.

These substitutions show and tell these scenes' entanglements. They might affect, or effect, who we are, and how we work. They might affect, or effect, how we study religion.

They do, in *Equus*'s case. These entanglements affect our ways of studying *Equus*, with terms, in our scenes.

Equus engages so many of religion's terms. They include *belief, body, classification, cognition, comparison, conflict, culture, definition, deprivation, discourse, emotion, exchange, experience, gender, god, hybridization, ideology, image, initiation, interpretation, liberation, manifestation, materiality, modernity, myth, narrative, origin, performance, person, play, priest, projection, rationality, relevance, ritual, sacred, sacrifice, salvation, structure, time, tradition, transformation, transgression, value, world, writing.*[7]

(Imagine these terms on a blackboard, or on a handout. In Intro, they might be. Imagine how we might arrange these terms. Imagine lines we might draw connecting them.)

These terms aren't enough. *Equus* calls for different terms, in this case. And *Equus* tests our terms, and our ways of using them—and us.

1.7

PROBLEMS

A CASE MEANS PROBLEMS. Studying a case means studying the problems it makes.

Studying a case in Intro means starting with problems. We start studying what we call religion by studying problems.

These problems pose test-questions, for us. They might unsettle us. They will displace us. A case's problems make us move: into a case's territory, onto a case's stage. They make us act, on their terms.

A case's problems act, too. They perform, pedagogically, *things are complicated in this case*—and *this case complicates things*.[1]

Equus does. It's a problem-play.[2] This play presents particular problems for studying religion. It recasts religion and studying religion, as problems, in this case.

We'll zoom in on problems of counting and of performance. This pair of problems poses plenty of test-questions.

How might we count religion(s) in *Equus*? What in *Equus* might we count as a religion?

How many religions might we count in *Equus*? How many theisms, and kinds of theisms, might we count in *Equus*? Might these counts (of religions and theisms) differ?

Would we count Alan's Equus-worship as a religion? Would we count an exclusive relation, of one divinity with only one devotee, as a religion? What kind of religion might we count it as (if we count it as one)? New? Hybrid? Temporary? Private? (Can a religion be private?)

With these counting questions come others.

How might we account for our counts, our decisions, in this case? How might *Equus* prompt us to re-count what we call religion?

How might *Equus* count? What might count for *Equus*? What might *Equus* value?

Mental health? Psychotherapy?[3] Normality? Abnormality? Imagination? Freedom? Fidelity? Sexuality? Passion? Pain? Extremity? Worship? Divinity? Divinicide? Sacrifice? Tragedy? Transgression? Transformation?

Each response is possible, for someone in *Equus*—and, maybe, for *Equus*. (Each response might also become a critical term for studying *Equus*.)

How about for us? Which responses might we count as possibilities?

It's a real, open question.

Factoring in performance problems multiplies our questions.

How might we stage *Equus*? What sort of play might we make it? (Might we stage it as a metaplay?)[4]

What kind of theatre might we make *Equus*?[5] Naturalistic? Cruel, following Antonin Artaud?[6] Epic, following Bertold Brecht?[7] A combination, somehow?[8] A different kind?

How closely might a production of *Equus* follow *Equus*'s scripted designs (set, lighting, sound, costumes, casting, etc.)?[9] How innovative might a production of *Equus* be? How might innovations affect *Equus*'s effects?

How might a performance of *Equus* feel?

How might these performative problems affect our ways of studying *Equus*? How might they affect our ways of studying religion?

That's a lot of questions. *Equus* poses a lot of problems. We might keep three more in view as we go. They're big, interpretive problems in this case.

Who might *Equus* be about?

Might anyone be sacrificed in *Equus*?

How might we make sense of *Equus*'s ending?

How we respond to these three problems might change everything about this case.

1.8

QUESTION

WHY ME?

This little question plays big parts in *Equus*. Equus asks it to Dysart. Dysart asks it to himself. *Equus* asks it to us.

Why Me?

This question comes in the opening scene of *Equus*'s second act. Alan and Nugget part, after their sexual, ritual night-ride. "Now he's gone off to rest," Dysart tells us, "leaving me alone with Equus" (§22/73). (Which, I wonder, is "he"?)

That stages an encounter: of Dysart and Equus, human and divinity. But Equus doesn't appear onstage. Equus remains invisible, transcendent. Yet Equus is present to Dysart. Equus exists in Dysart's reality.

Equus calls to Dysart. When Dysart responds, peering into a psyche (his or Alan's), "there he [Equus] is," Dysart tells us, "waiting for me" (§22/73). Dysart stares at Equus staring at him.

Figures like Equus, Dysart tells us, "precede us" (§22/74). They're in the scene before we are. We arrive and encounter them. We're exposed to them.

Suddenly, a figure captivates us. It captures us. "Moments," Dysart tells us, "snap together like magnets, forging a chain of shackles. Why?" (§22/74)[1]

That's Equus's question to Dysart: "Why Me? . . . Why—ultimately—Me?" (§22/73) Why does Equus capture Alan? Why does Equus captivate Dysart? *Why Equus*?

"I don't know," Dysart tells us, "nor does anyone else" (§22/74). Dysart admits his limits, his limitations. He knows he can't know how to respond to Equus. Dysart knows he can't, in Equus's words, "totally, infallibly, inevitably account for Me" (§22/74).[2]

We can't, either. Whatever else this scene might enact, it might enact, for us, a pedagogical lesson. We might learn lessons about studying religion.

Why Me? is what things Dysart investigates ask him. It's what things we investigate ask us. These things, in *Equus*'s case, include horses, humans, divinities, affinities, relations, devotions, practices, norms, values, of and in a religion. (This listing is partial.)

Why might these things count for a religion? Why might a religion count these things as valuable? Why might we? Why *these* things, in *this* case?[3]

We might learn, like Dysart, to admit our epistemic and explanatory limits. We might, like Dysart, admit them, self-consciously and self-critically.[4] We might learn from Dysart that we can respond to *Why Me*? only partially.

And we might learn with Dysart that we can't uncover origins. Like Dysart, we can study a magnetization's effects. We can't access the moment of magnetization.

A magnetization's "chain of shackles" might be the "sharp chain" in Dysart's final lines: "There is now, in my mouth, this sharp chain. And it never comes out" (§35/110). If so, then Dysart's lines might be about our situations, as humans. They might be lines about what it means to be a human.

Why Me? continues to call us. It questions us, professionally and personally. *Why Me*? asks us why we study what, and how, we study. Why study this religion? Or why study this part of this religion?

Or, more immediately, why study this play? Why this case?

I feel how personal these questions are. I feel my vulnerability in responding to them. It's as if I'm alone onstage, in a dark performance-space, with a spotlight on me.

But responding is important. It's part of being a self-conscious, self-critical student of religion. It's part of demonstrating that we're in the performance we call studying religion.

Why Me? *Equus* asks me.

My response has morphed over time. I'm sure it'll morph again. Here's my response, for now.

Equus magnetizes me. It fascinates and frustrates me. *Equus* won't stay still. My senses of *Equus* (especially its ending) change each time we interact.

I keep questioning *Equus*. And *Equus* keeps questioning me.

Equus keeps me questioning.

That's partly because *Equus* is a play. A play multiplies interpretive possibilities and complexities. It involves textual and embodied and performative and effective interpretations. Changing one of them changes the others. They can keep changing. A play keeps itself in play. And it makes us part of the performance.

It's also partly because *Equus* is religiously ambivalent. Would I count *Equus* as a demonstration of religion's significances? Would I count *Equus* as a criticism of religion and its effects?

I can't decide. *Equus* works either way—or both ways. It works as demonstration *and* criticism, tangled together.

That works well pedagogically. And it captivates me. And it makes me aware of what and how I count when I study religion.

Equus also complicates studying religion. It doesn't fit into existing frames. It escapes usual ways of containing, and studying, religion. *Equus* calls for doing things differently.

To study *Equus*, as a student of religion, I'm bound to imagine, experiment, invent, innovate. That excites me. It opens possibilities. I get to reimagine what naming and studying religion might involve. In Intro, I get to do that with students.

Plus *Equus* is a wild ride. It gallops across delimitations. I enjoy hanging on.

ACT 2

2.1

STAGING

WE'RE HERE FOR A PERFORMANCE. Let's imagine our ways into one.

Already, we have questions.

A performance of what?

When and where?

By whom?

For whom?

How?

Why?

Our questions are specific. They remind us that a performance is *a* performance. It's specifically situated: in bodies, in relations, in contexts, in space-times. (Bodies are situations, too.)[1]

These situations matter. They affect how a performance materializes and makes sense. They affect how performers, a performance, and its audience interact.

So let's imagine our ways into a specific, situated performance: of *Equus*, produced by the National Theatre, in London, in 1973. That's the production *Equus*'s published text describes.

This performance's set is spare. It's only, Peter Shaffer writes, "a square of wood set on a circle of wood" (3), plus some benches.

This set makes us imagine. We must imagine it differently, in different scenes. It becomes Dysart's office, or the Strangs' living room, or Alan's hospital room, or a stable, or a field.[2] And we must imagine props, like the Manbit and the hoof-pick.

Even if we're reading *Equus*, we need to imagine its performance. When we read a play, we stage it, in our imaginations. For a play, reading becomes reading-staging.

Our imagining involves us in this performance. It needs us: to imagine. It's a part we're playing, as spectactors.[3]

This performance's staging puts us onstage. Spectactors sit upstage, in blocks of tiered seats, separated by a tunnel. That would make this performance of *Equus* happen between an audience. We would watch both: a performance and part of an audience watching a performance. And they would watch us watching.[4]

Through this staging, we might imagine ourselves into other performative roles: other relations with Dysart and Alan and *Equus*.[5]

We might play medical doctors or students. The stage would become, Peter Shaffer writes, "a dissecting theatre" (4). That would cast Dysart and us as physicians. It would cast Alan as a corpse. *Equus* would perform a postmortem. Our role would be to observe, and confirm the pathology.

We might play psychology students. The stage would become a classroom. Dysart would become our teacher. Alan would become our subject, or object, of study. *Equus* would perform a pedagogical lesson. Our role would be to learn from Dysart.

We might play psychotherapists. The stage would become an office. Dysart would become our patient. Alan would become a topic. *Equus* would perform a psychotherapeutic session. Our role would be to treat Dysart.

We might play judges (human or divine). The stage would become a courtroom. Dysart would become a witness, or a defendant. Alan would become a victim, or an exhibit. *Equus* would perform a trial. Our role would be to render judgment.

We might play ritual observers, or ritual participants. The stage would become a ritual space. Dysart would become a ritual celebrant. Alan would become a ritual subject, or object. *Equus* would perform a ritual (maybe an exorcism, or a sacrifice, or something else). Our role would be to take part.

We might play confessors. The stage would become a confessional. Dysart would become our confessant. Alan would become a transgression. *Equus* would perform a penitential rite. Our role would be to hear Dysart's confession—and, maybe, to absolve.

We might play a chorus.[6] The stage would become a stage. Dysart and Alan would become character-actors. *Equus* would perform a play, or a metaplay. Our role would be to watch.

Playing different roles would involve us in different scenarios, different perspectives, different relations. They would give us different ways of making sense of *Equus*.

Imagining ourselves into different roles, we'd reimagine *Equus*'s performances. (*Equus* might perform in more-than-one ways.)

Which role(s) might we play? Which staging(s) might we choose?

That would depend: on a performance, and on us.

It might depend on different embodiments, of *Equus*'s players.[7] It might depend on how we interact (experience, interpret, relate) with their embodiments of abilities, ethnicities, races, genders, sexualities. It might depend on different performative affects, and affective relations, and acting choices.

(How, for example, might we make sense of Dysart's performance? As cold? Detached? Professional? Solicitous? Resigned? Didactic? Desperate? Broken? Brokenhearted? Destroyed? Destroying? Dead-in-life?)

Whatever a performance might do, it would do something. It would make differences. We'd have to interact with them.

2.2

PERFORMANCE-TEXT

PERFORMANCE CHANGES A PLAY. It changes how we might make sense of a play.

Performance prevents us from reducing a play to a text: a script. That's a way of containing. It's a way of sacralizing. It protects a text from embodiments. And it keeps our readings trained on meaning, or on narrative. But meaning isn't a play's prime mover.[1] Neither is narrative.

For a play, our ways of reading change. Reading becomes reading-staging. That recasts us: as dramaturgs, designers, directors, actors, spectactors.

(How might these roles change how we make sense of *Equus*? What if you or I were *Equus*'s costume designer? Or its sound director? Or an actor playing Nugget? Or a spectactor in a Broadway theatre? Or a spectactor in a Kenyan theatre?)

So *reading* might not be the best word for what we do with a play. *Studying* might be better. *Relating* might be even better. *Interacting* might be better still. Let's go with *interacting*.

A play is an interacting: of performance and text.[2] It's both, together. They're inseparable as a play.[3]

Let's call a play a performance-text. That marks their inseparability, with a hyphen.

A performance-text's hyphen is a chiasm.[4] It's a crisscrossing, an interchange. Chiasmically, performance and text supplement each other.[5] They mediate each other. A performance-text's hyphen doubly binds performance and text.

And it makes a chiasmic double passage. This hyphen crisscrosses territories and borders of performance and text.[6] It crisscrosses through imaginations and realizations.

A performance-text's hyphen crisscrosses genres, too. They include literary genres, performative genres, corporeal genres, relational genres, spatio-temporal genres, ontological genres.

Equus's performance-text chiasm crisscrosses genres of realism and ritual, of intimacy and theatricality and metatheatricality. It crisscrosses kinship relations and therapeutic relations and erotic relations and religious relations. It crisscrosses horses, humans, and divinities.[7] *Equus*'s performance-text chiasm crisscrosses through its players, and their interactions, and their effects. And it crisscrosses through us.

A performance-text mixes genres.

No, it shows us mixed genres.[8] It shows us that genres mix, intermix: that they're mixtures. (That makes them more-than-ones.) And mixing or mixed genres mix up genres. They become crossings, chiasms.

In *Equus*'s case, these mixed genres include what we call disciplines. That reminds us that *Equus* would work differently in different terms: of literary studies, or performance studies, or religious studies.

These studies have crossable borders. We should cross them.[9]

2.3

INTER-

A PERFORMANCE-TEXT IS *INTER*-.[1] It happens in between: through its hyphen. It happens through its hyphenate interactions and interchanges. A performance-text *is* interactions and interchanges.

A performance-text is a complicating interchange of interpretations.

Some interpretations are textual. Let's call them interpretations.

Other interpretations are performative. Let's call them translations.[2] They translate a text, and interpretations of it, into a performance.[3]

That involves bodies. For a performance-text, translations are bodily praxes. Bodies perform a performance-text. And bodies watch (or, if they're reading-staging, imagine) bodies perform a performance-text.

Then we make sense of these interpretive translations, or translated interpretations. Like any translation, these have to work. They have to make sense to us, so that we can make sense of them.

Equus is especially interchanging. It's made of *inter*- things. And it makes things *inter*-.

Equus does so, directly, through Dysart. He's intersubjective. He moves through his subjectivity, Alan's subjectivity, Equus's subjectivity, maybe Nugget's subjectivity, and their intersubjective interactions.

In Alan's reenacted night-ride scenes, Dysart acts as inquirer. He wants to know more, professionally and personally. He wants to learn more, about Alan and his religion. So Dysart asks Alan questions, to solicit disclosures.

That's how Dysart learns about, and gains a way into, Equus-religion. Dysart learns about its divinity, Equus. He learns about its mythology, of divine opponents and salvific sacrifice, and its legal code, Straw Law. Dysart learns about its night-ride's ritual calendar (one ride every three weeks) and ritual objects (sandals of majesty, chinkle-chankle, Manbit). He learns about its ritual practices: touching, feeding, disrobing, riding, merging, orgasming.

We learn, with Dysart, that Equus-religion is an interreligion. Equus-religion incorporates Christian elements, like a divine father-son relation, a last supper, a self-sacrificing-for-salvation divinity, a mystical possibility of human-divine union. Equus-religion incorporates other elements, too. They come from stories Dora reads to Alan, and from Alan's experiences and Alan's imagination.

So Equus-religion isn't a version of Christianity. But Equus-religion isn't possible without parts of Christianity. Equus-religion is *and* isn't a new religion. It's an interreligion. (For us, that poses problems of comparison. An interreligion is intracomparative.)

By *Equus*'s end, Dysart enters Equus-religion. In Alan's last stable scene, Dysart acts as inquisitor. He plays a divinity, interrogating Alan. Dysart speaks as Equus. His questions aren't really questions. They're prompts, for Alan's abreaction. That reenacts Alan's horse-blinding act: of, maybe, equicide and divinicide.

Dysart also inhabits Alan's performative acts, directed at him. Alan's stares perform accusations: "*At least I galloped*! *When did you*?" (§25/81) Dysart loops Alan intersubjectively into his internal dialogue. He plays both parts.

Dysart's intersubjective interactions are with us, too. Dysart is interreal.[4] He moves between realities: Alan's, his, ours. And he addresses us. That's how *Equus* begins and ends.

Dysart's direct addresses are interactive and interchanging. And they're interpellating.[5] They hail us. They implicate us. They incorporate us in *Equus*, across realities (its and ours).

Dysart interpellates us by addressing us. Or *Equus* interpellates us through Dysart's addresses. Dysart is *Equus*'s interpellating apparatus.

Through Dysart, *Equus* enacts—*is*—an interpellating address to us. It interpellates *us*, individually and collectively. And *us* includes our embodiments and our embodied differences.

Through its interpellations, *Equus* interanimates itself, as a play and a metaplay. Dysart's addresses don't let us forget that *Equus* is a play.

2.4

MASK

MASKS DON'T LET US FORGET, either: that *Equus* is a play.

Masks are part of *Equus*'s interworkings. They play important parts.

Masks are crucial to Dysart's dream. He dreams himself high priest at a ritual sacrifice of children. He's wearing a ceremonial mask. Then the mask slips. The other priests see Dysart's green, sweaty face. "They tear the knife," Dysart tells us, "out of my hand . . . and I wake up" (§5/18).[1]

Dysart's dream-mask works dialectically. It sets up an opposition of concealing and revealing. This dialectic is manifest. We get it. We're meant to, I think.

I'm more interested in other masks in *Equus*: masks that show up on *Equus*'s stage. They're the masks the horse-actors wear.

These masks are made, Peter Shaffer writes, "of alternating bands of silver wire and leather; their eyes are outlined by leather blinkers" (5). (That's how these masks were made in the National Theatre's 1973 production. Most productions have followed its lead.) The horse-actors' human heads, Shaffer writes, "are seen beneath them [the masks]. No attempt should be made to conceal them [their heads]" (5).[2]

We see through these masks. We're meant to.

We see through a dialectic of concealing and revealing. These horse-masks don't conceal or reveal. They do neither. And they do both.

These masks cast *Equus*'s horse-actors as just that: horse-actors (hyphenated). They figure these horse-actors as interspecies players. These horse-actors are performing chiasms. Their masks make them: horse-actors.

It happens ritually. We watch these horse-actors perform this chiasm, in an onstage ritual. They put their masks on together, with us watching them, and them watching one another. Their masking, Peter Shaffer writes, "has an exact and ceremonial effect" (5).[3]

We see through these masks. So this ritual—theatrical, or religious, or a mixture—isn't transformative. It's interformative. These horse-actors remain interspecies. They enact this hyphen.

We see and imagine them. We imagine them as horses.[4] And we see them, through their masks, as humans playing horses. We see them playing.

They play through movement, not mimesis. These horse-actors stand upright. They don't crouch on all fours. They never neigh or whinny. These horse-actors enact equine effects with their bodily movements.[5]

What if they play only through movements? What if these horse-actors don't wear horse-masks?[6] Might this unmasking of *Equus* change almost everything about *Equus*?

(Think about what *Equus* might look like, in performance, without horse-masks. Think about what that might do to our senses of *Equus*. Think about how much more *Equus*'s performance without horse-masks might need us: to imagine.)

How might these performative differences affect *Equus*: its senses, interpretations, translations, receptions?

Equus's unmasking might point us in four different ways (among others).

(1) Without horse-masks, we would see only horse-actors' bodies and embodiments. Performative movements would make them interbodies and interembodiments. They would make human bodies move as horse bodies.

That would spotlight embodied differences. It would spotlight their ways of embodying differences: from one another, and from us, and from other animals.[7] We might see these differences through their horse-masks. Unmasked, we can't miss them.

These differences might unmask our assumptions about embodied differences. We might see how we value different bodies, and how we value bodies differently. Doing so might also unmask our humanisms, our anthropocentrisms, our other *-isms*.

(2) This unmasking might—especially for us, studying religion—unmask other senses of religion in *Equus*. We might see them through Dysart's dream-mask. This mask is part of a religious ritual: an ancient Greek sacrifice. That directs us to think about ancient Greek religions' roles in *Equus*. (They might not all show up onstage.)

Masking and unmasking play vital roles in many ancient Greek mystery religions. Mystery religions, their divinities, and their human-divine relations remain masked to uninitiates. Entry into a mystery religion enacts an initiating ritual. It unmasks divinity to humanity, in intimate relation. A divinity like Dionysos would reveal himself to votaries: humans devoted to him.[8]

A divinity like Equus would do the same, to his single votary. Might we reimagine, or reexamine, Equus-religion as a new mystery religion?

(3) This unmasking might—especially for us, studying religion—recall some of *Equus*'s critical moments. They're moments when *Equus* invokes some of religion's critics.

Karl Marx, Friedrich Nietzsche, and Sigmund Freud act in *Equus*. Alan cites Marx's "Religion is the opium of the people" (§6/22). Dysart alludes to Nietzsche's "God is dead" when he tells Alan that gods die (§27/86). And *Equus* is full of psychotherapeutic scenes. In different ways, *Equus* performs this trio's criticisms of religion.

These criticisms are unmaskings. Marx, Nietzsche, and Freud unmask religion as a drug, as a crypt, as a phantasy.[9] They unmask religion as dehumanizing. We can see religion through their criticisms. We might see *Equus* as unmasking religion—differently.

(4) This unmasking might return us to Dysart, via horse-masks. I think Dysart's most interesting mask isn't his dream-mask. It's a sort of horse-mask.

Dysart's interspecies horse-mask isn't really a mask. It's a horse's head Dysart feels himself wear: invisible, but real. "You see," Dysart tells us, "I'm wearing that horse's head myself. That's the feeling" (§1/10).

No, we don't see. So we have to imagine it, because Dysart does.

2.5

PLAY

WE'RE STUDYING *EQUUS*.

We're studying religion.

We're already in play.

We're in play with our imaginations, our senses, our methods, our problems, our terms, our values, our realities.[1] *We're* in play, too.

Play moves us—and *us*. It gets us moving. It keeps us moving. It keeps us open.

(I'm focusing, in this scene, on play as a praxis. If you'd like, you could insert an *a* before every *play*. It would work either way.)

Play is movements: of possibilities, of differences they might make.[2] Play names a way of unfixing. Its ends are unforeseeable. And play keeps things incongruous. That makes play unmappable—unless we map as we play.

Play doesn't ensconce us in a safe space. In play, nothing is safe-and-sound.[3] Play pushes things, including us, to edges. It exposes our edges: of sensing, making sense, knowing.

That's where learning happens. We learn on edges, at limits, of what we already know. These edges are porous.

And play's bounds are pliable.[4] Play frames us with a Möbius band. It loops inside and outside. It twists them together. In play, inside and outside intermix. Play *is* interplay.[5]

In our case, it's an interplay of performance and critique. An act in play might be either. Or it might be both. It can act multiply, at once.

Play's effects, like learning's, don't stay bounded.[6] So play, like learning, is risky. It makes differences. We can't stop their movements, their effects.

We're in play in a theatre, as part of a performative scene. We're in play in a class, as part of a pedagogical scene. We're part of what's happening in these scenes.

We're part of what's happening in *Equus*'s scenes. And playing with *Equus* means playing with Dysart, and Alan, and Equus, and ourselves. We're all in play in each of *Equus*'s scenes. *Equus* is playing fourways.

All four of us are in play in *Equus*'s pivotal act: Alan's horse-blinding. So are different realities, and different possibilities of making sense. Alan's act puts them in play.

In Hesther's, or Frank's, or Jill's, or Dalton's realities, Alan's horse-blinding might make sense psychologically. (In Hesther's and Dalton's realities, it might also make sense criminally.) It might make sense as an act of someone psychologically afflicted.

But this sense might provoke different responses. With Hesther, it might provoke sympathy. With others, it might provoke bewilderment, or outrage, or horror, or a combination of them.

Alan's horse-blinding might make different senses.

In Alan's reality, it might make sense religiously, as a double act: of sacrifice and salvation. Alan's horse-blinding might sacrifice Equus to save Alan. (Equus won't save Alan.) Alan might sacrifice his divinity, and his religion, to save himself from both. Or Alan might sacrifice his relations with Equus, and with horses, to save possibilities of other relations, with humans.

If Alan's horse-blinding is a sacrifice, it's an ambivalent sacrifice. Alan might (also) desire to sacrifice himself, to save himself from living without equine relations.

That might be why, after Alan blinds the horses with a hoof-pick, he stabs at his eyes with it. It might be why Alan tells the hoof-pick, "Find me! . . . Find me! . . . KILL ME! . . . KILL ME!" (§34/107) Alan's salvation might also be Alan's destruction.

In Dora's reality, Alan's horse-blinding might make different religious sense. It might make sense diabolically, as an act of the Devil. "He was my little Alan," Dora tells Dysart, "and then the Devil came" (§23/77). The Devil is responsible, not Alan. That's what Dora believes. Or that's what Dora needs to believe.

In Dysart's reality, Alan's horse-blinding might make sense multiply.

It might make professional sense, psychotherapeutically.

It might make private sense, passionately.

It might make priestly sense. Dysart, a psychiatrist, is a priest of the Normal. The Normal, Dysart tells us, "is the indispensable, murderous God of Health, and I am his priest" (§19/62). Dysart's Normal-religion, like Alan's Equus-religion, is an exclusive monotheism. Neither can abide another divinity.

Dysart's priestly duty would be to see to Equus's death. Alan's horse-blinding might effect Equus's murder, or sacrifice. Or it might signal Dysart to murder Equus: by treating Alan.[7]

How might we make sense of Alan's horse-blinding act? Maybe we find ourselves in one of these players' realities, these ways of making sense. Maybe we imagine our ways into one, or more than one. Maybe we take other ways, make other senses of Alan's act.

Our decisions wouldn't take these possibilities out of play. Questions of sense don't close because we make decisions.

How we make sense is in play.

Play makes us decide among possible senses.[8] They're valued possibilities. In play, we learn to decide. And we learn to examine how and why we decide.[9] In play, we learn ways of critical inquiry. They're ways of making sense.

If we make sense of Alan's horse-blinding in terms of religion, what are our deciding terms? What if we decide to use other terms? How might different terms make different sense?

How might our decisions about terms, senses, realities expose our decision-making methods, values, norms, limits? How might they expose us? How might we respond to our exposure?

What if we take our exposure seriously? What if we let it—ourselves—be in play? What might we learn from this play?

2.6

ACTING

HERE I AM, ACTING.

What might that mean? What am I doing here?[1]

Am I *really* acting? Or am I really *acting*?

Am I doing something real? Or something imaginal?

Yes. Acting is interacting between what we call real and what we call imaginal. Acting plays between them. It con-fuses them.

I do: I act: I perform. These colons mark interactions. They enact intertwinings. These colons remind us that what we call real and what we call imaginal come con-fused. What we call imagination is real. It acts in reality. Imagination makes real differences.

So does literature. So does religion.[2] So does performance. They act, they do things, with imagination.

We do, too. We act. We act *as if*. Acting is acting *as if*.[3] We act *as if* our acting will do something. We act *as if* our acting will make differences, in our realities. We act with real imagination.

As if translates imagination's *what if...*? into action. So does an aesthetic. So does an ethic. So does a belief. *As if* intertwines aesthetics and ethics and beliefs and realities, with imagination.[4]

As if is how we decide how to act. It's critical to an ethic.[5] An ethic depends on *as if*.

Imagine I encounter an ethical problem. I'm called to act. How? How do I decide how to act?

I imagine my possible actions, in this situation, *as if* they happened. I imagine what my possible actions might do. I imagine their possible effects. (To imagine these things, I imagine myself between possible presents and possible futures.)

I valuate these different imagined effects. I judge which effects I might count as ethical. I judge and count them in terms of a virtue, or a duty, or a calculation, or a care, or a responsibility.[6]

Then I decide how to act.

Then I decide to act.[7]

Then I act.

By acting, I enact a virtue. Or I do my duty. Or I calculate. Or I care. Or I realize my responsibility. I perform, ethically. I step into an ethical scene, and I act. I act *as if* my act will make a difference in this scene. (I need to believe that it will.)

So does Dysart. So does the actor playing Dysart.

For Dysart, treating Alan is an ethical problem. How should Dysart act? What should Dysart do?

Equus asks these ethical questions. They're dramatic questions, too.

In *Equus*, we watch Dysart go through a process like the one I (imaginarily) went through. We watch Dysart work through *as if* possibilities: with Hesther, with himself, with us. And we watch Dysart perform ethical acts and counteracts in *Equus*'s last scene.

First, Dysart promises Alan: "It's all over" (§35/107). Equus will, Dysart tells Alan, "go away now. You'll never see him again, I promise" (§35/107). Dysart promises Alan release from Equus's chains, and the pain they inflict.

Then Dysart tells Alan the truth. The truth is: Dysart is lying. The truth is: Dysart can't promise what he's promised. Equus, Dysart tells Alan, "won't really go that easily" (§35/108). Equus might not go at all. And "when Equus leaves—if he leaves," Dysart tells Alan, "it will be with your intestines in his teeth" (§35/108). Losing Equus, Alan will lose some of himself.

Then Dysart advises Alan. "If you knew anything," Dysart tells Alan, "you'd get up this minute and run from me fast as you could" (§35/108). Dysart's advice to Alan is: go, end this treatment, keep galloping, hang on to Equus's reins and the passion (and pain) that entails.

Then Dysart agrees to take Equus away. Dysart will treat Alan. Alan will, Dysart tells us, "be delivered from madness" (§35/108).

Which act(s) does Dysart judge ethical? Why counteract them, with others?

We're called to respond, to make sense of *Equus*. To respond, we would have to imagine ourselves into Dysart's role, and imaginatively act *as if* we were Dysart.

An actor playing Dysart is called to respond, too: to make performative sense of *Equus*. How might this actor respond? How might this actor perform these responses?

How might these performative responses, and our senses of them, affect a performance of *Equus*? What differences might they make, for *Equus* and for us? What differences might they make if this actor's responses to these questions differ from ours?

These questions, of ethics and interpretations and performative translations, open other questions. They're big ones.

When do you think Dysart decides to act as he finally does: to take Equus away from Alan, or to take Alan away from Equus? (Which is it, do you think?) Maybe it's when Dysart says, finally, "*All right*! *I'll take it away*" (§35/108). Maybe it's when Dysart promises Alan "it's all over" (§35/107). Maybe it's earlier in *Equus*. (When?)

How you respond would make differences, ethically and interpretively and performatively.

If Dysart decides before "*All right*," then for at least some of *Equus*, he's acting *as if* this ethical question remains in play. And "*All right*" becomes performatively different: a declaration, not a decision.

If Dysart is decided from the start—if he's determined to disentangle Alan and Equus—then *Equus* enacts a different ethical performance. Determinism, not decision, drives *Equus*'s acts.[8]

How might these ethical differences affect our senses of *Equus*'s tragedy? If tragedy comes from collisions of ethical possibilities, how might ethical differences make *Equus*'s tragedy different?[9]

And what about *Equus*'s ending? Which is it, do you think: does Dysart take Equus away from Alan, or Alan away from Equus? Do you think Alan's treatment—Dysart's treatment of Alan—kills Equus? Or do you think Equus survives?

Either way, these questions return us to Dysart's mysterious last lines: "There is now, in my mouth, this sharp chain. And it never comes out" (§35/110). How might ethics and their performative effects alter our senses of these lines?

Studying *Equus*, you and I are acting *as if* we have a sense of these last lines, their meanings, their effects. But how many *as ifs* are still in play, in these lines, for us?

2.7

MAKE-BELIEVE

LITERATURE, LIKE RELIGION, calls for believing.

Literature, like religion, appeals to us: *believe me.*

We might ask: *why*?

Because, literature responds, *you have to.*[1] *If you don't*, literature adds, *I won't work.*

Literature, like religion, needs believing. It depends on our *yes* to its appeal: *you have to believe me.*

We might ask: *how*?

By believing, literature responds: *by imagining your ways into my realities, and by acting as if they were real, for you—as if they were yours.* Or literature might respond: *by giving my realities credit, as if they counted for you.*[2]

Believing is acting *as if.*[3] It's enacting *as if.* Believing is performative.

And believing is interacting *as if.* Believing is a relation—an ethical one. It's a way of relating with *some other.*[4] (In this case, literature is *some other.*) By believing, in relation, we say *yes*, performatively, to *some other.*[5] We affirm our relation, across our differences.[6] We make believing happen.

Believing is make-believing.

And make-believing is making-believe.

That goes for literature, or religion, or science, or whatever we call reality.[7]

Make-believing denatures believing. It recognizes that believing counts on *as if.* It grants imagining's role in believing. And make-believing admits that we make believing, and that we make believing happen.

When we make-believe, we act: on desire and decision.

Desire drives make-believe. To make-believe, we have to want to make-believe. We have to want to crisscross realities, to act *as if* some other realities are real for us.

And we have to enact our desire. To make-believe, we have to decide to make-believe. Make-believing decides on our desire: to act *as if.* Our decision to make-believe makes us believe. It activates our believing, performatively.

When we make-believe, we make *as if* realities real, for us. We make-believe them real by making-believe in them.

Making-believe engages our aesthetics. It animates our phenomenologies. It stretches our epistemologies. It probes our ethics. And making-believe tangles them, together, with imagination and credibility.

That opens our present realities. It presents, in this opening, a counter-present.

Counter- doesn't oppose. It supplements. It makes an other way. It adds differences. And making-believe depends on differences.

In a counter-present, making-believe re-presents imagination's question. *What if our present, our reality, were different*? *What if this counter-present were ours*?

Literature presents us with these questions. A play, a performance-text, enacts these questions. And it responds, by enacting a counter-present. A performance-text puts a counter-present in play, with us, in performance. And it asks us to make-believe in it.

A religion does, too. A religion depends on make-believe: on acting *as if*. Without make-believing, a religion won't work.[8] A religion needs make-believe. It needs us to make-believe in it.

That's what *Equus* needs, too, in more ways than one.

Make-believe me, *Equus* appeals: *make-believe in my realities.*

Make-believe me, Alan appeals: *make-believe in my religion, in my realities.*

Make-believe me, Dysart appeals: *make-believe in my story, in my realities.*

Make-believe me, Equus appeals: *make-believe in me.*

Make-believe me, they appeal, *as if my realities are yours.*

That's a play's appeal, to us. (A performance-text embodies this appeal.) It's a performative and pedagogical appeal, for us. A play activates a practicum in making-believe. That turns a theatre, or a classroom, into a laboratory for studying making-believe.

Imagine we're interacting with *Equus* in performance. What happens?

Equus begins with two actors. They come onstage. One is, probably, a young man. The other is, probably, wearing a horse-mask. They stop, together, in a spotlight. They stand, touching. What happens next would depend on a performance.

Maybe the human-actor's arms wrap around the horse-actor. Maybe the human-actor's hands caress the horse-actor's chest, or shoulders, or neck, or face-mask. Maybe the human-actor's face nuzzles the horse-actor's chest, or neck, or cheek. Maybe the horse-actor reciprocates the human-actor's nuzzle. Maybe the horse-actor doesn't.

Maybe they stand, touching, for a moment. Maybe they stand, touching, for a while.

When *Equus* begins, that's what happens—until we make-believe.

When we make-believe, things change.

Making-believe in *Equus*'s opening, we see Alan and Nugget, a young man and a horse. We see their interactions, their intimacy. We recognize their romance. We watch a human-horse embrace.

We hear Dysart tell us that's what we're watching. "With one particular horse, called Nugget," Dysart tells us, "he [Alan] embraces" (§1/9). The horse, Dysart tells us, "digs its sweaty brow into his cheek, and they stand in the dark for an hour—like a necking couple" (§1/9). Dysart's words (help) make us believe what we're making-believe.

Making-believe, we watch *Equus*.

We watch Alan and Nugget.

We watch Dysart and Hesther.

We watch Alan's and Dysart's psychotherapeutic sessions.

We watch the Strangs' family dynamics.

We watch Alan's and Equus's relations. We watch Alan's rituals, in his bedroom and in the Field of Ha Ha.

We watch Alan and Jill, in the stable. We watch Alan feel watched by Equus. We watch Alan blind six horses.

We watch Alan and Dysart come undone.

We watch a religion's invention, its enactments, its effects, maybe its undoing.

We act *as if* these things are happening. We enter *Equus*'s realities. Or they enter ours. Either way, realities crisscross. They interact. Maybe these interactions affect us. Maybe they affect our realities.

Maybe they affect how we study religion. Making-believe in a play can make ways for studying religion.

(That's one reason we study plays in Intro. And it's why, in Intro, we perform scenes from plays we study. Making-believe works performatively.)

We might study how our making-believe in *Equus* works. We might analyze how it works on us. We might examine how purposive or passive our decisions to make-believe were, or are.

We might study what our making-believe does. We might test its effects, and how long they last.

And we might study our making-believe critically: knowing that we're making-believe.

2.8

PLAY-IN-PLAY

LET'S STEP BACK, and survey the scene.

Equus opens with make-believe. It opens with Dysart's making-believe a scene, of Alan and Nugget. Dysart make-believes it out of what Alan showed and told him.

So *Equus* begins with showing. It shows us into Dysart's make-believe. Then Dysart tells us about it. He addresses us, directly, from stage.[1] When he does, things shift. We shift into different relations, in different realities.

These plurals count. Our shifts double our relations, our realities.

We're in our realities, interacting with *Equus*, as spectactors. And we're in *Equus*'s realities, in a performance, as players. We're, in reality, bi-situated. We're in two places, two roles, in this performative scene.

And we know it. We're making-believe in *Equus*'s realities. And we know we're making-believe in *Equus*'s realities, in ours.

Equus performs its realities *in our realities*. (They're our everyday realities: the ones we make-believe in every day.) *Equus* enacts plays-in-play of realities.[2]

Equus must make sense to us, in both realities' terms. Otherwise, we won't be able to make-believe in *Equus, as if* its realities are ours—at least for a while. Then *Equus* won't work.

Dysart reminds us of our multireal situation(s), from the stage.

Dysart reminds us in *Equus*'s opening scene. He reminds us when he recounts his dream, about child-sacrificing and mask-slipping. He reminds us when he describes the Normal. Dysart reminds us when he's asked, and asks, *Why Me*? And Dysart reminds us when he tells us how he's going to treat Alan.

All five reminder-scenes are monologues Dysart delivers, to us. All five shift us abruptly, across realities.

These five scenes are *Equus*'s most metaperformative scenes. They remind us that *Equus* is a performance-text, one we're making-believe in. And they offer commentaries on this performance-text from within it.

These five scenes are the only scenes in *Equus*'s present. Everything else in *Equus* happens in a flashback (or, sometimes, a flashback-in-a-flashback).

And everything in *Equus* comes from and through Dysart: in a play-in-play, scripted and staged by him. *Equus* is Dysart's story. It's a story Dysart shows and tells us, dramatically. Dysart's is, really, *Equus*'s only voice.

Dysart plays, metaperformatively, *Equus*'s entire production team. He acts as writer, producer, stage manager, dramaturg, designer, director, narrator, character. Dysart decides what gets staged, and how.

So Dysart, through *Equus*, appeals, to us: *make-believe me, as if you trust me. Make-believe me*, Dysart appeals, *as if* Equus, *this story I'm showing and telling you, is enacting my testimony.*

Would we? Would we make-believe in Dysart? Would we trust him?

Whatever we decide, Dysart's appeal reminds us that fiction and testimony, imagination and reality, come entwined.[3] It reminds us that believing involves make-believing. We act *as if* something is true or real.

Like *Equus*, like literature, like religion, testimony or truth or reality calls for acts of making-believe. It calls for our decisions to make-believe *as if* it's true or real. And it calls for us to do so knowingly: taking a critical step back.

It's a step of critique.

Critique operates through, and as, play-in-play. Critique *is* questioning. It *is* frame-shifting. Critique requires that we be in more reality-frames than one, at once.[4]

That's because critique involves, and involves us in, ways of valuing ways of valuing. (That's my sense of critique.) Critique involves, self-critically, ways of valuing *our* ways of valuing.

Critique is performative and metaperformative. It stages plays-in-play. And critique is möbiatic, too. It keeps us twisting, in its questioning bands.

ACT 3

3.

I

CASTING

LET'S RETURN TO THE STAGE.

Imagine that you're staging a performance of *Equus*. How might you cast *Equus*? Who might you cast as Alan? As Dora and Frank? As Dysart? As Jill? As Nugget? Who might be in your dream cast of *Equus*?

Take a minute to imagine.

Casting involves envisioning *Equus* in performance, in bodies, onstage.[1] So it involves bodies and their differences. Different bodies would corporealize *Equus* differently. Different corporealizations would affect, and effect, *Equus* differently. They would make differences, for *Equus*'s actors and spectactors.

What differences might you want this performance of *Equus* to make?

In other words, how might you imagine this performance of *Equus*?

Maybe you imagine it historically. Maybe you want to reproduce the National Theatre's 1973 production.

Or maybe you imagine this performance currently: in your reality. Maybe you want to situate *Equus* in your space-time, in your current cultural contexts. *Cultural* would involve *religious* and *secular*. (How might a performance of *Equus* change if it re-accounted for secularizations and their effects? How might a performance of *Equus* be different in a secular, or a postsecular, situation?)

Or maybe you imagine this performance transformatively. Maybe you want to reimagine *Equus*, making different production decisions. Maybe they include different casting decisions: about abilities, ethnicities, genders, races, sexualities of *Equus*'s players.[2]

What if you cast a man as Jill? Or a woman as Nugget?

What if you cast a Black man as Dysart? Or a Black woman? Or a trans Latinx actor? Or a disabled South Asian actor?[3]

What if you cast the Strangs multiracially? What if, with your casting, there's no genetic way that Alan might be Dora and Frank's biological child? How might racial differences affect other differences among the Strangs?

What if Dora, Frank, Jill, and Dalton doubled as horse-actors?[4]

How might different castings change *Equus*? How might different bodies make different sense of *Equus*? How might they make *Equus* make sense differently?

Take another minute to recall your dream cast of *Equus*. Would you make the same dream-decisions?

How might you decide? How might you make casting decisions? Why? And when? Would you decide these things before casting? Or based on casting sessions?

How, for you, might casting decisions, interpretations, and translations of *Equus* interact?

What about other production decisions? How might you design, set, light, costume, stage *Equus*?

What might your stage's shape be? Would you seat spectactors onstage? Would you keep *Equus*'s cast onstage for the entire performance?

Would your set be minimal? Would it reproduce the National Theatre's design? Would you use material or imaginal props? Furniture? (A hoof-pick?)

What would your horse-actors wear? Would they wear horse-masks?

What would the Equus noise in your production sound like?

What theories, of acting or performance or religion, might you draw from?

What sort of performance might you stage *Equus* as? A tragedy? A mystery? A family drama? A love story? A ritual? A ritual sacrifice?

What kinds of acting performances might you want? Realistic? Surrealistic? Ritualistic?

How might Alan act? Might he seem fragile? Reverential? Scared? Desperate? Angry? Other things?

Where onstage would you position Alan when he reenacts his bedroom ritual? Behind Frank and Dysart? Above them, on some sort of platform? To one side of them? In front of them? Would Alan face spectactors? (How fiercely would he beat himself with his coat hanger?)

How might you treat Alan's nudity in the stable scenes? How might you light these scenes, to affect what spectactors might see?

What other questions might you ask about materializing *Equus* in a performance? How might your responses materialize *Equus* differently?

So many questions, I know. But questions are critical. They make ways for differences.

Keep questioning, and responding, and reimagining. Keep asking *What if . . . ? What if things were different*?

3.2

RELATIONS

I'M EXPOSED.

And I'm not alone.

I'm performing this couple of sentences right now.[1] You are, too. We live through this couple of sentences.

This couple of sentences is how we are: in relation.[2] It's who we are: in relations.

Relations are plurals. They're matters of more-than-oneness, or of one-moreness.

Relations inhere in us. We inhere in relations. We find ourselves, always, in relations. Relations make and unmake and remake us.

But relations aren't things. They're acts. Relations name exposing interactions, with differences. They mean vulnerabilities.

A performance or a pedagogy, of almost any kind, enacts this scene's opening couple of sentences. Ways of performing, and ways of interacting, and ways of learning are ways of relations.

A religion is, too. A religion is a way of relating—especially if a religion is a way of connecting and communing. Relations make up a religion. (A practice, a ritual, a belief, a text, a divinity: they all name relations.)

And they make up *Equus*. *Equus*—including everybody in *Equus* and everybody interacting with *Equus*—is in relations.

Equus opens in relations. It opens with *with*. *With* is *Equus*'s opening word, in both acts. It's "*with* one particular horse, called Nugget," Dysart shows and tells us, that "he [Alan] embraces" (§1/9, §22/73). And it's *with* this horse-human couple that Dysart make-believes himself and us. These relations make our ways into *Equus*.

Equus is full, maybe overfull, of relations. They include familial, professional, imaginal, erotic, sexual, devotional, religious, and ritual relations.

Some are interpersonal. Some are interspecies. Some are binding, and some aren't. Some ravel, and some unravel.

Different relations have different effects.[3] These effects might empower. They might overpower. They might seduce, deceive, reveal, help, consume, sacrifice, and/or save those they relate.

All of *Equus*'s relations move through Alan. Dysart is *Equus*'s narrative nexus. But Alan is *Equus*'s relational nexus. He's *Equus*'s relational interchange. Every player in *Equus* relates to, and through, Alan. Every relation in *Equus* happens through, and because of, Alan.

I'm focusing, for now, on *Equus*'s familial relations.[4] I listed them first for a reason. Familial relations are there before us.

Plus *Equus*'s familial relations frame *Equus*'s other relations. The Strangs' relations enmesh familial and religious relations. They show us, onstage, that religious relations and kinship relations come together.[5]

For the Strangs, kinship relations are religious relations. Kinship positions come bound with religious convictions. *Christian* is bound to *mother. Atheist* is bound to *father*. (Might we hyphenate them: Christian-mother and atheist-father?)

Among the Strangs, fights between *mother* and *father*, over *son*, are about religion. "Bloody religion," Frank tells Dysart, "it's our only real problem in this house, but it's insuperable" (§7/28).

Religion informs Dora and Frank's parental practices. Differences between their parental practices *are* religious differences.

Alan seems to want out of these parental-religious relations and their effects. Or maybe he wants to replace them: with other relations.

That might be one reason Alan wishes he were a cowboy. "I bet," Alan tells Dysart's tape recorder, "all cowboys are *orphans*!" (§13/44) "No one," Alan tells Dysart's tape recorder, "ever says to cowboys 'Receive my meaning,'" as Frank does, or "'God's got eyes everywhere,'" as Dora does: "they wouldn't dare" (§13/44).

Cowboys, Alan imagines, can tie their own kinship knots.

Maybe that's what Alan hopes his Equus-religion will do: tie kinship knots differently. Maybe Alan tries to undo kinship relations by redoing religious relations. Or maybe Alan tries to replace kinship relations with religious relations.[6] Maybe that's why Equus-religion gives so much attention to genealogies, with "those begats" (§14/46).

Might a religion be a way—maybe a different way—of kinship?

Alan might try to swap Equus for Dora and Frank. Equus would replace mother and father. (That would short-circuit a Freudian scheme.) This replacement would mix parental relations with erotic, sexual, mystical relations. Equus would become a divine parent-replacement that Alan wants to merge with: ritually, sexually, mystically, ontologically.

Or Alan might try to displace parent-child relations with partner relations. That would displace one kind of kinship with another. Alan's displacing partner might be a fusion of Equus, a horse-divinity, and Nugget, a horse. Equus and Nugget would intermix. So would Alan's relations.

These relations are queerly interrupting, and queerly confusing.[7]

By unworking or reworking kinship through religion, kinship would become suprahuman. Alan would tie kinship in human-divine, and human-equine, relations. And he would tie human-divine, and human-equine, relations in kinship.[8]

3.3

IMAGE

IN ALAN'S BEDROOM, on a wall, at the foot of his bed, hangs an image. It's torn down. Then a different image is hung in its place.

This sequence plays out many of *Equus*'s relational and religious differences. They condense and collide. That makes these two images key players in *Equus*. *Equus*, in many ways, turns on these images.

Both images are extreme. So are relations they affect, and acts they effect. As Dysart reminds us, "Extremity's the point" (§25/79).

The first image is of Christ en route to Calvary. This Christ, Dora tells Dysart, "was loaded down with chains" (§11/39). "And the centurions," Dora adds, "were really laying on the stripes" (§11/39).[1] This image is Christian. And it's sadomasochistic. And in terms of Dora and Frank's fights about religion, it's an image of Dora's victory.

Following one of these fights, Frank tears down this image. Alan cries for days. So Frank gives Alan another image. (Without Dora and Frank's fights, this exchange of images wouldn't have happened.) Alan hangs it, Dora tells Dysart, "in exactly the same position" (§11/40): in his bedroom, on a wall, at the foot of his bed.

The second image is of a horse. It's a photograph taken head-on. "It comes out," Dora tells Dysart, "all eyes" (§11/40). They stare directly at you.

Imagine what that might look like.

(In a performance, we wouldn't see these images. We'd have to imagine them, from Dora's descriptions. But what if we saw the second image, when we see—through Frank's eyes—Alan's bedroom ritual? And what if, instead of a horse, it imaged the horse-actor playing Nugget?)

A horse-image hangs where a Christ-image hung. That seems so simple. I don't think it is—not for us, studying religion. This image-change opens questions about religion in *Equus*. And it opens questions about studying religion in, or through, *Equus*.

What happens, religiously, in this image-change? How might we make sense of it? As a replacement? Or a substitution?

A substitution, to me, suggests a stand-in. It's temporary. A substitution wouldn't change a desire. It would reroute it, for now.

If a horse-image substitutes for a Christ-image, it might be just a substitution of images: images, not divinities. A substitution might make Alan's Equus-religion a bizarre kind of Christianity. But Alan's Equus-religion wouldn't count as a new or different religion.

A replacement, to me, suggests something more permanent. A replacement isn't a stand-in, for now. It's a lasting difference. It would change a desire (among other things).

If a horse-image replaces a Christ-image, it might signal a religious replacement. That replacement might, in this case, be necessary. Frank's tearing down the Christ-image might enact a death of god.[2] And the death of a god would enact, for Alan, the death of a religion. Alan might be crying in mourning, for his divinity and his religion, both now dead.

The replacing horse-image might image a different divinity.[3] That would call, for Alan, for a different religion. Alan would have to make it up, using available elements and his imagination and his desires.

So substituting images would mean a religious modulation. Replacing images would mean a religious innovation. Either way would mean, for us, questions of comparison.[4]

A substitution would raise questions of intrareligious comparisons. How might we compare modulations, variations, within a religion's frame? How flexible, how expansive, might this frame be? How many modulations or variations might a religion accommodate? How much difference would be too much? Who would decide, using which measures?

A replacement would raise questions of interreligious comparisons. They would be particular, in this case. This case is a comparative problem.

Alan's Equus-religion incorporates Christian elements. It combines them with other elements. So Alan's Equus-religion wouldn't count as Christianity, or a variation of it. But Equus-religion wouldn't be imaginable without Christianity, or elements from it.

Equus-religion would *and* wouldn't be a new religion. It would count as an interreligion. It would be, already, comparative. In this case, comparison would stage itself, in *and*. *And* would make new ways of thinking through, and doing, what we call comparison.

Let's return to Alan's bedroom, and to the horse-image: head-on, all eyes, staring.

Eyes are major players in *Equus*. They seduce and they surveil. They make some things happen and keep some things from happening. Eyes, equine or divine or both, are what Alan stabs—blinds—maybe kills—with a hoof-pick.[5]

Eyes' roles make *Equus* a performance-text about seeing: about meanings of seeing.[6] It's about who sees, who's seen, who can't see, who won't see. And it's about how these visioning differences matter.

That includes our seeing, as we interact with *Equus*—a performance we're part of. What kind of performative act might watching be?[7] Who or what are we watching when we watch a performance? Might that include us?

What might *Equus* be teaching us about seeing? How might *Equus* be teaching us to see, or to see differently? Maybe *Equus* performs, for us, a pedagogy of seeing. That might be one of its metaperformative loops.

3.4

HUMAN-HORSE-DIVINITY

WHO OR WHAT DO YOU THINK *Equus* is about?

Is *Equus*, do you think, about a *who* or a *what*?

Let's devise some responses, to these two meaning-full questions: of *Equus*, for us.[1]

Maybe *Equus* is about relations across kinships and religions. Then *Equus* might be about Alan, Dora, Frank, Equus, maybe Nugget, and their interactions. Dysart might be more narrator than character-actor.

Or maybe *Equus* is about Dysart. Then *Equus* might be about psychotherapy and its effects, or passion's importance for humans, or chasms between desiring and acting, or the price of the Normal.

Or maybe *Equus* is about Alan. Then *Equus* might be about a human-horse couple, or links between familial and imaginal lives, or a make-believed religion, or the price of the Normal.

Or maybe *Equus* is about how one act (like image-replacing or horse-blinding) can change lives—including who lives, and how.

Or maybe *Equus* is about someone or something else. We could keep devising responses.

(In Intro, we would. We'd keep devising responses until we couldn't think of any more. We'd find lines in *Equus* to support our responses. We'd probably use our handout of terms. Our responses might become term-based. We might write our responses on the board. And we'd explore what interpretive, performative differences our responses might make.)

Let's devise one more response, for now. What if our response were: human-horse-divinity?

Who or what might that mean? Might it mean a *who* (or *whos*) or a *what*? Which might count more: the terms or the hyphens? What might these hyphens mark?

They might mark interdevelopments. They might mark interdomestications, or interdependencies, through histories. Humans and horses have, for centuries, interrelated.[2]

Horses have played integral roles in how humans have made and remade things. These things include humans, horses, other animals, divinities, religions, realities, communications, cultures, agricultures, industries, colonies, wars. Without horses, these things wouldn't have become who or what they are. Neither would we.[3]

So human-horse seems to name, for us, an inextricable interrelation.[4] That might make it difficult, maybe impossible, to disentangle these species.[5]

It would be in Alan's case. Alan tries to embody this interspecies interrelation. "He is trying," Dysart tells Hesther, "to *become one*" (§25/81): a human-horse hybrid.[6]

Or he's trying to become a horse, through religious rituals.

In his bedroom ritual, Alan imagines morphing into a horse.[7] His ritual ends with his self-bridling, using a piece of string. Then Alan thrashes himself with a coat hanger.

In his night-ride ritual, Alan gallops toward mystical fusion, with Nugget-Equus. "I want to BE you," Alan exclaims to Equus, "forever and ever!" (§21/71) Alan rides, frantically, toward ritual-mystical climax. He shouts to Equus, "Make us One Person! *One Person*! *One Person*! *One Person*! *One Person*!" (§21/72)

Alan aims, ritually, to become an interspecies, divinized, three-in-one *who*: human-horse-divinity. These hyphens would mark mixing, merging, melding interchanges. They would mark religious intercourses.

Human-horse-divinity might be an interweaving way of naming Alan, in (as?) relational interactions. Or it might be a complicating way of naming Dysart.

Dysart is, from *Equus*'s opening, interspecies. He's already human-horse.[8] "That's the feeling," Dysart tells us: "I'm wearing that horse's head myself" (§1/10).[9] And "I," Dysart tells us, "keep thinking about the *horse*!" (§1/9)

Who? Nugget? Dysart? Dysart make-believed as Nugget?

Whose horse-head might Dysart imagine "kissing him [Alan] with its chained mouth" (§1/9)? Who is "nudging through the metal some desire absolutely irrelevant to filling its belly or propagating its own kind" (§1/9)?

Might it be Dysart? Might this through-the-metal desire be Dysart's: "to jump clean-hoofed on to a whole new track of being I only suspect is there" (§1/10)?

Dysart might be a human-horse, subject to a horse-divinity. If Alan is a human who wants to become divine by becoming equine, Dysart might be a human who has become equine, subject to a divinity.

Equus is in Dysart's horse-head. Dysart can't stop hearing Equus. Equus doesn't stop interrogating Dysart: "Why Me?" (§22/73, §35/109) Dysart, wearing a horse-head and hearing Equus's question, might be whom human-horse-divinity names.

Or human-horse-divinity might name Equus. Equus is a horse-divinity make-believed by a devoted human.

So *who*, then?

What interpretive, performative differences might *who* make?

What religious differences might *who* make?

3.5

DEVOTION

WORSHIP SATURATES *EQUUS*. *Equus* is dripping with worship.[1]

Worship might make our academic antennae buzz. We recognize it, as one of religion's terms. And we recognize it as one of *Equus*'s terms.

Worship might be what powers *Equus*. Worship—a question of worship—might be *Equus*'s fulcrum.

"Can you think of anything worse one could do to anybody than take away their worship?" (§25/79)

That's Dysart's question: to Hesther, and to himself, and to us.

Nonsense, Hesther might respond. Hesther interprets Alan's horse-blinding act in psychological, not religious, terms. To Hesther, worship isn't Alan's (or *Equus*'s) problem. Pain is. "The boy's in pain," Hesther tells Dysart: "That's all I see" (§25/82). And Dysart, Hesther believes, can take away Alan's pain.

No, Dysart seems to respond, *I can't*. Dysart values worship as vital. "Without worship," Dysart tells Hesther, "you shrink" (§25/81). Your life shrinks. Dysart's has. And, Dysart believes, Alan's will.

Dysart figures worship as an extreme way of living. Alan "lives," Dysart tells Hesther, "*one hour* every three weeks—howling in a mist" (§25/79). Alan lives when he worships Equus, on horseback. Alan's ritual riding performs his living worship. In it, Alan addresses—and sends—himself, totally, to Equus. Alan gives himself to Equus, ritually and mystically and sexually.

Our academic antennae might be buzzing again. That might prompt us to question Dysart's question.

What might Dysart count as *worship*?

How would *one* take away *anybody*'s worship? Would worship be something take-awayable? Would taking it away be once and for all?

Would Dysart assume that *anybody* worships? Would worship be, functionally, ubiquitous? (If so, how could *one* take it away?) Would worship, for Dysart, be a religious act: an act of, and contained by, a religion?

These questions raise problems for us. And they return us to Dysart's question. For us, it might become *Equus*'s question.

"Can *you* think of anything worse one could do to anybody than take away their worship?" (§25/79)[2]

Well, can you? Dysart and *Equus* ask us.

They address and interpellate us. They call for our response.

And they remind us that worship is a question of value. Worship *is* a way of enacting value.

It's not the only way. It's not the only act of living in extreme, limit-pushing ways. Yet worship, in Dysart's sense, seems to try containing these ways within what we call religion.

What if we change terms? What if we change *worship* to *devotion*?

What if Dysart's question becomes "Can you think of anything worse one could do to anybody than take away their devotion?"

Worship is an act of devotion. But devotion isn't delimited to specific acts, or to religious confines.

Devotion names a praxis. And it opens to other kinds of interrelations. They might include ethical, or existential, or erotic ones. They might include interrelations like commitment, or dedication, or fidelity. These interrelations might or might not be bound by religion.

So devotion would trouble, and twist, limitations we call religious or secular. They're limitations worship likely leaves untroubled.

Plus devotion, in English, adds linguistic twists.

An act of worship works, grammatically, as *I worship* ______: subject act object. An act of devotion works, grammatically, as *I devote myself to* ______: subject act reflexive-pronoun preposition object. Devotion takes a reflexive turn. It includes *myself*. And devotion points to, not at, its object.

This reflexive turn makes devotion grammatically irreversible. *I worship* ______ can reverse itself, passively, into ______ *is worshipped by me*. But *I devote myself to* ______ can't be reversed so easily. It doesn't have a corresponding passive form.

Maybe that's because devotion is an action and a passion. Neither is confinable to *an* act.

These verbal differences make nominal differences. A worshipp*er* worships. A devot*ee* devotes. *Devotee*'s suffix marks this power differential. It marks a devotee's power deficit. The subject, or object, of devotion has the power.

Devotion, instead of worship, would open ways for us to figure *Equus* differently.

I don't think Alan worships Nugget. But Alan, I think, is devoted to Nugget. He might be as powerfully (though differently) devoted to Nugget as he is to Equus. These devotions might intersect, or interact, or even conflict.

They'd loop through religion. But they wouldn't be limited to, or by, what we call religion. Or they'd loop other things, like desire and sexuality, into what we call religion.[3]

I don't think Dysart worships Alan or Equus. But Dysart is devoted to Alan. (By *Equus*'s mysterious last lines, Dysart might be devoted to Equus.) That's what makes Dysart's dilemma so agonizing. It's part of what makes *Equus*'s end so devastating. Devotion can be: devastating.

3.6

SEXUALITY

ALAN, IN HIS NIGHT-RIDE RITUAL, has sex with a horse. (You knew that was coming.)

How might we make sense of this sex-act? And of Alan's sexuality?

We can't rely on our usual letter-boxes. Alan's sexuality won't fit into any one of them. It crosses, and crisscrosses, our usual ways of counting sexuality. It denatures, and denaturalizes, sexuality.[1] Alan's sexuality shows us how unstable, and destabilizing, sexuality might be. Alan's sexuality is, for us, so complicating. (That's why I'm spotlighting it in this scene.)

Sexuality complicates you or me. It complicates who *you* or *me*, or *we*, might name. Sexuality might be your, or my, or our doing *and* undoing.[2]

(Might religion be, too?)

Maybe that's because sexuality isn't a thing. It's relations—interrelations. What we call sexuality names situated, interchanging relations among desires and passions, pleasures and bodies, identities and orientations, acts and practices, powers and knowledges, kinships and values, ourselves and others.[3] It names ways we live through these relations.

(Might that also name what we call religion?)

These relations interrelate. And they're malleable. They—and, so, we—can morph.

Usually, these relations are exclusively human. So are our usual senses of sexuality. They stop at human boundaries.

Sexuality, especially Alan's, exposes our relational limits. It exposes us, sexually, as usually humanistic and anthropocentric.[4]

Alan's sexuality isn't so limited. It doesn't stop at human boundaries. Alan's sexuality crosses, and fissures, these boundaries. It exposes these boundaries as fissures.[5]

Alan's sexuality is extreme. It's interspecies. And it's three-way (at least).

Each of Alan's sexualized interactions in *Equus* involves Alan, a horse, and at least one other.

One interaction, on a beach, involves Alan, Trojan, and the Horseman. Another encounter, in a stable, involves Alan, Nugget, and Jill. Another interaction, in a field, involves Alan, Nugget, and Equus. One more interaction, back in the stable, involves Alan, Nugget, Jill, Equus, and five other horses—plus (in its reenactment) Dysart and (in its performance) us.

In a different interaction, in Alan's bedroom, Alan plays two roles: human and horse. This interaction involves Alan, Equus, and Alan-made-equine. In this sexualized scene, Alan is interspecies. And human-Alan beats equine-Alan with a coat hanger.

(These horses are all masculine. Incidentally? Or integrally for Alan's sexuality?)

In the Strangs' home, religion and sexuality come entangled.[6] Alan learns from Dora "that sex," Dora tells Dysart and Frank, "is not *just* a biological matter, but spiritual as well" (§7/28). And Frank thinks religion, he tells Dora and Dysart, "is just bad sex" (§7/28).

Religion and sexuality get entangled for Alan, too. But Alan's entangling is different: from theirs and, probably, from ours.

Religion's and sexuality's entanglements might be what *Equus* is about.[7] And untangling religion and sexuality might be what Dysart does in *Equus*'s final scene. The way to untangle Alan and Equus might be to untangle religion and sexuality. This untangling would be Alan's undoing.

For Alan tangles religion and sexuality tightly. His night-ride enacts this tangling. Alan's sexuality becomes ritualized and ritually enacted: with denuding, props (like the Manbit), BDSM power-plays, bareback riding.

Who does Alan ride? Who does Alan desire? Nugget? Equus? Nugget-Equus?

And what does Alan desire? Penetration? Fusion? Transformation?

Alan, in his night-ride, might want all of the above (maybe sequentially, maybe simultaneously).

As Alan rides, bareback and nude, he shouts, "I'm stiff! Stiff in the wind! *My* mane, stiff in the wind! *My* flanks! *My* hooves!" (21/71)

Then Alan cries, "I'm raw! Raw! Feel me on you! *On* you! *On* you! *On* you! I want to be *in* you. I want to BE you forever and ever!" (§21/71)[8]

Then Alan screams, "Make us One Person! *One Person*! *One Person*! *One Person*! *One Person*!" (§21/72) Then Alan trumpets, onomatopoetically: "HA-HA! HA-HA! HA-HA! HA!" (§21/72)[9] Then Alan orgasms.

How many are in this scene? Three? Two? One?
And what happens among them?
And how might we name what happens, in sexuality's or religion's terms?
(Can we?)

3.7

QUEER

WHATEVER ELSE *EQUUS* MIGHT BE, it's queer.

It's queerly sexual. And it's queerly religious. Sexuality and religion come queerly together in *Equus*.

That makes me wonder: in *Equus*'s case, how many things are sexuality and religion? How might we count sexuality and religion in *Equus*? How might that affect how we count sexuality when we study religion?

These questions of counting are queer ones.

What might that mean? What might they mean?

Here's my way of responding. Others would respond differently. You might be among them.

(In this scene, like a few others, I'm standing downstage. I'm addressing myself to you—as in a monologue.)

Queer insists on counting sexuality. It insists, really, on counting sexualities. Queer reminds us that sexuality is, always, sexualities.

Queer isn't only sexual. We can't extricate sexualities so easily from other things, including our bodies. Our corporealities keep our sexualities bound to other embodied differences.[1]

But queer and sexual remain twisted together. Queer means in relations to sexualities. It ensures that sexualities keep counting.

And it names different ways of counting sexualities. Queer pluralizes possibilities. It diversifies things. (It diversifies diversities.) Queer makes way for living differences.

What if things were different? Imagination's question is a queer one.

It keeps asking us about differences. It keeps us asking about differences.

Queer coils us into its questions. It makes us into questions. That's queer's critical move. It's how queer threads critique: through itself and us.

Queer's questioning disrupts things. Queer works with prefixes, like *un*- and *de*-, *counter*- and *re*-, *inter*- and *trans*-. Queer might undo things. It might redo things. It might destabilize or counteract things. It might make things *inter-* or *trans-*, with their moving hyphens.[2]

These things might include us.[3]

That's risky.

So is queer. It's not safe-and-sound. It's exposing. It's denuding.

Queer denudes us. It bares *us*.

Queer strips us of fixities. It exposes them as real fictions: fictions we like to call realities. Queer denatures our preset norms, our precalculations.[4] With queer, we can't count on ready-mades.

Queer fissures things.[5] Then it passes, and lets other things pass, through these fissures.

Queer exposes, and examines, our ways of making sense. It questions our ways of counting, knowing, deciding, acting, living.[6] And it keeps questioning.

We remain open: to critical questions, and to different responses. Queer does, too. Queer is part of its critical, questioning performance.[7]

What if this performance were a way of studying religion?

What if how we study religion is queerly?

What if we name, or count, religion queerly?

In *Equus*'s case, I think we should. Alan's religious praxes are sexual. And his sexual praxes are bound with religion. They're, religiously, doubly bound: with Alan's Equus-religion, and with Dysart's Normal-religion.

What about in other cases? What if we work queerly in terms of studying religion? What might that do, or undo?

3.8

NUDE

I'M EXPOSED.

And I'm not alone.

Alan performs these interrelated sentences. Near *Equus*'s end, he embodies them: nude onstage, with Jill, in the stable.

(That poses questions of performance. Would Alan denude himself? Would Jill denude Alan? How readily or reticently? How long might this denuding take? And how might this scene be lit? To minimize or maximize character-actors' exposure and vulnerability?)

Alan stands nude—denuded: before Jill, Equus, Nugget, five other horses, Dysart, and us. Alan is nude for the rest of *Equus*.

Imagine the exposure. Imagine the vulnerability.[1]

These nude scenes are and aren't Alan's first. Alan denudes himself as part of his night-ride ritual, with Nugget and Equus. (So denuding is part of Alan's Equus-religion.) But when Alan reenacts this scene, he doesn't denude his body. He pretends to. Alan, *Equus* tells us, "*mimes undressing completely in front of the horse*" (§21/68).

Later, when Alan reenacts the stable scenes, he doesn't mime denuding. He performs it.

Alan is then doubly nude: physically and psychologically. Alan's physical denuding materializes his psychological denuding. They happen together, finally, in a therapy-ritual. They perform, together, Alan's total exposure.[2]

Dysart conducts this therapy-ritual, as a priest of the Normal. Normal-religion and its divinity demand psychological denudings. They insist on submissions, confessions, sacrifices.

These acts are Normal-religion's prices. They might be other religions' prices. And they might be too high.

Are they? That's one of *Equus*'s questions, to us. Other questions follow.

What if they are? How might that affect how a devotee enacts a religion? How might that affect how we study religion?

And which prices are higher: Equus-religion's or Normal-religion's?

Let's return to Alan's nude body, bared onstage.

Nude returns us to bodies. It recalls us to their singular materialities. And these materialities are differences. They're different for every body. They're different for any body. (Our bodies self-differ over time: as cells are replaced, as we're materially recomposed, as we grow and age.)

Nude singularizes and situates a body. A nude body is *this* body, in *this* situation. *This* nude body isn't any other. It's singularly different.

This nude body exposes differences of ability, ethnicity, gender, race, sexuality. And it exposes other, singular differences, like a birthmark, or a musculature, or a pigment variation, or a scar. They're singularly material differences, exposed.

Exposure names a performative relation.[3] Nude does, too. This nude body *is* in relations.[4] And it performs *here's my body, singularly, exposed and vulnerable, to you*. It does so intimately, each time.

When Alan denudes himself, Jill watches. Nugget and five other horses watch. Equus watches. Dysart watches. We watch.

For us, Alan's denuding scene might have multiperformative effects.

This denuding scene might immerse us in it. It might submerge us in *Equus*'s make-believed realities. We might sense how exposed, how vulnerable, Alan's body is.

Or this denuding scene might fissure realities: *Equus*'s and ours. It might hurl us into corporeal sensitivity. It might remind us that we're watching a make-believed performance. We might sense how exposed, how vulnerable, this actor's body is.

In this scene, we might see the body of Alan, nude, in a stable.

We might see the body of an actor playing Alan, nude, on a stage.

We might see both.

Whose eyes might we be seeing through? Ours? A horse's? Dysart's?

What if they were divine eyes? Might this scene cast us as a divinity: as Equus, or the Normal? Might that make us complicit in Alan's denuding?

Or might that turn these divine eyes on us? Might we, through them, cast critical eyes on ourselves?

ACT 4

4. I

DIRECTING

EQUUS CALLS US INTO QUESTIONS. They're questions about it, and about us. They're questions about our senses and our relations: about how we make them, and how they make us.

These questions, and their effects, make *Equus* a critical performance-text for us, for studying religion. (But *Equus* can't contain these questions or effects. That's critical, too.)

Let's consider some of these questions in translation: from text to performance.

Imagine that you're directing a performance of *Equus*. You're translating, from page to stage. So you're responding to *Equus*'s questions, and others that follow.

Imagine *Equus*'s opening scene. Imagine your stage. It might be bare, and only spotlit. Or the lights might glow, warmly or coolly. Maybe there's even machined fog.

Alan and Nugget might be alone onstage. Or they might have a chorus of actors, watching them. Maybe these actors are playing us. Maybe we're playing them.

The horse-actor playing Nugget might wear a horse-mask. Nugget and Alan's interactions might seem attentive, or tender, or transgressive. One or the other might seem the more powerful player.

Spectactors might sense that Alan and Nugget are more than boy and horse. This scene might play like a love scene, or like a farewell scene, between a boy and his horse-boyfriend.

How long would you have this scene run, before Dysart speaks?

When he does, where might he look? How might he sound? How might Dysart be trying, hoping, to affect spectactors?

As *Equus*'s director, you'd decide which questions to ask about this scene.

You'd decide, with your actors, which responses to offer. Your performance of *Equus* would perform your decisions.

Maybe you'd cast *Equus* across abilities, ethnicities, genders, races, sexualities. Maybe you'd use casting to trouble the Strangs' kinship relations, or to suggest other kinships. (What if twins played Alan and Nugget?) Maybe you'd put a horse-image, or a horse-actor image, in Alan's bedroom scenes.

Maybe you'd want Frank to seem sincere, or overblown, or icy.

Maybe you'd want Dora's monologue, about Alan and the Devil, to seem like words from a caring, broken mother—or like a filial abandonment.

Maybe you'd want Jill to seduce a reluctant, or an eager, Alan.

Moving through *Equus*, moment by performative moment, you'd make so many decisions. They'd make, or remake, *Equus* in performance.

And they'd be guided by other decisions, about some big questions.

Who is *Equus* about?

What is *Equus* about?

What does *Equus* value?

How does *Equus* look, sound, feel?

What happens at *Equus*'s end?

What might happen to us after *Equus* has ended?

As *Equus*'s director, you'd direct others through your responses. You'd also be directed: by *Equus*. So you'd be directing *Equus*, and *Equus* would be directing you. You'd give each other directions. Directing *Equus* goes both ways.

It goes in other ways, too, based on other interactions. Your designers would bring their imaginings into the performance-space. Your actors would bring their bodies, and their performances, onstage. Your spectactors would bring their senses, their ways of making sense, into the performance-space.

For me, teaching is a lot like directing. I'm directing and directed. I move between my senses and others' senses of what we're studying. These moves are performative and pedagogical. They're making ways for learning, for us.

How might you act as a teacher-director? What kind of teacher-director might you be?

Would you respond to these big questions about *Equus* before meeting with designers and actors—or students? Or in meetings and rehearsals—or classes? How malleable would you let your responses be?

Would your senses of what we call religion come before, or from, *Equus*? How case-based would these senses be? How revisable would they be?

Maybe you'd decide, before meeting with designers or actors or students, that *Equus* is about Dysart, and about a psychotherapeutically ritualized killing.

Maybe you'd decide, during rehearsals or classes, that *Equus* is about Alan, and about passions' perils.

You might decide that *Equus* is about Equus, and about religions' persistent powers.

Or you might decide that *Equus* is about imbrications of sexuality and religion, or about a queerly multiple love story, or about humans' mistreatments of other animals, or about psychotherapy's failures, or about a question of devotion, or about a metacommentary on performance.

(Or you might decide that *Equus* is about one, or more, of this book's scene-titling terms.)

Maybe you'd decide different things.

Whatever you decide would refigure *Equus*. Your decisions would refocus *Equus* on, and around, specific scenes. They would materialize *Equus* differently. They would change *Equus*'s performance: what it performs, and how.

4.2

PASSION

PASSIONS MIGHT BE what powers *Equus*. They wind their ways through its religious, secular, sexual relations. Passions drive characters, their actions and interactions. And they spur devotions.

A passion befalls Alan. It happens *to* him. It's an event—an extreme one.

A passion overtakes Alan. It acts on him. Alan acts through it.

A passion dislodges and displaces Alan. It moves him. A passion pushes Alan, and his realities, to their limits. They're his limits. In his realities, they're possibility's limits. A passion pushes on possibility. (A religion does, too.)

A passion impels its subject to limits. It's an experience of limits. It's a question, a questioning, of limits.[1]

At limits, a passion binds Alan. It's a knotted event.[2] (It's another knot.)

A passion binds Alan to horses. "They," Alan tells Dysart's tape recorder, "sort of pulled me. I couldn't take my eyes off them" (§13/44).

For Alan, a passion's binds are made of bridles. They're bridles Alan wears. A passion holds the reins. It doesn't let go.

An equine-passion reins Alan, singularly, to one horse: Nugget. This passionate relation is erotic. And it's ritualized. Nugget is a vital part of Alan's night-ride ritual.

An equine-divine passion reins Alan, singularly, to one horse-divinity: Equus. This impassioned relation is religious. And it's sexual. And it's overpowering.

These passions, for Nugget and for Equus, are knotted. They cross in Alan. They crisscross through Alan into a complex equino-religious passion.

This equino-religious passion prevents Alan from having sex with Jill. "Every time I kissed her," Alan tells Dysart, "*He* [Equus] was in the way" (§33/103). Alan's Equus-passion renders him impotent with humans. It allows Alan only human-horse-divine intersexions. Even while with Jill,

Alan tells Dysart, "I wanted the foam off his neck. His sweaty hide. Not flesh. *Hide*! *Horsehide*!" (§33/103)

This passion is too much for Alan. Bound to limits, Alan can't endure there.

A passion's knot doesn't hold. It's a double bind.[3] Its binding unbinds.

(So does an analysis. Analysis, of whatever sort, names a praxis of unbinding.[4] It's a way of undoing.)

Bound, Alan comes unbound.[5] He's turned inside out. Inside and outside pass into each other.[6]

A different sexualized passion might rein Frank. (It might be a passion. It might be something else. I'm not sure.) Frank's passion would be pornographic and collective. It would turn a pornography theatre into a ritualized place of passion. With other men, night after night, Frank would watch onscreen sex acts.

Frank's passion would push him to limits of authority: parental power. It would expose Frank, his passion and his limits, to Alan. Alan might see Frank as, Alan tells Dysart, "nothing special—just a poor old sod on his own" (§31/96). Or, Alan tells Dysart, he might see Frank as "just like me" (§31/97).

An other passion seems to befall Dysart. It's not the passion he tries to develop: for ancient Greece.

Dysart knows better. He knows that passion, he tells us, "cannot be created" (§35/109).

The passion that grips Dysart is for the passion that grips Alan. (It might be, by extension, for Equus. That might be what Dysart's mysterious last lines tell us.) This passion is vital, jealous, charging. Alan, Dysart tells Hesther, "has known a passion more ferocious than I have felt in any second of my life" (§25/80). And "let me tell you something," Dysart tells Hesther: "I envy it" (§25/80). Dysart passionately envies Alan's sexualized equino-religious passion(s).

Dysart might envy the extremity of the passion Alan experiences. He might envy its sexualized or religious qualities. Dysart's envy might reinforce *Equus*'s impassioned relations of religion and sexuality.[7]

(I haven't mentioned gender. But these three impassioned players are masculine. Might passion be gendered in *Equus*? How might gender, sexuality, passion, and religion interact in *Equus*?)

This passion makes Dysart feel indicted by Alan's stare. Dysart feels Alan's stare saying, performatively, "*At least I galloped*! *When did you*?" (§25/81)

But galloping passionately has a price. Dysart watches as an equino-sexual-religious passion consumes Alan. It makes Alan not want to live.

By *Equus*'s end, in some senses, Alan won't. A passion will destroy him. Or it will lead him to destroy himself. Or Dysart will destroy this passion. "Passion, you see," Dysart tells us, "can be destroyed by a doctor" (§35/109).

One way or another, the passion that Alan experiences will destroy him. Which way is Dysart's dilemma.

Should Dysart destroy this passion—and, so, destroy Alan?

Or should Dysart let this passion—let Equus—destroy Alan?

What differences would which way make? For whom?

4.3

PAIN

ALAN IS IN PAIN. That's *Equus*'s problem.

That's not my claim. It's *Equus*'s. *Equus* shows and tells us so.

Alan isn't the only one in pain. Dora is in pain. Frank is in pain. Jill is in pain. Nugget and five other horses are, eventually, in pain. Dysart is, enduringly, in pain.

But their pains aren't *Equus*'s problem. Alan's pain is. It's the problem *Equus* acts to solve.

Alan's pain first appears on *Equus*'s stage when Alan has a nightmare. His body contorts. He seems, *Equus* tells us, "*frantically straining to tug something back*" (§8/29). Then Alan cries out: "Ek! . . . Ek! . . . *Ek*!" (§8/29)

We would hear, see, feel Alan's pain in performance.[1] (If a performance seats *Equus*'s cast onstage, these character-actors would hear, see, feel it, too.) We would soon learn what "Ek!" means. We would soon figure out what Alan strains to tug back.

Equus's problem, Alan's pain, is a religious problem.[2] It complicates relations of religion and pain in *Equus*.

Before Equus, Alan has two religions. He has a received religion: Dora's Christianity. And he has a mediated religion: television.

(An updated performance of *Equus* might substitute digital screens—computers, tablets, phones, etc.—for televisual ones. I don't think this change would change Frank's message, or Dysart's at *Equus*'s end.)

Frank denounces both religions, as drugs. He forbids Alan to watch television. And he tears down Alan's image of Christ. Taking away Alan's religions causes Alan pain.

Or it allows Alan, drug-free, to feel pain. It takes away Alan's pain-management systems. "Religion," Frank (probably) tells Alan, "is the opium of the people" (§6/22). He's reciting Karl Marx. He's reciting Marx's criticism of religion as opium.[3]

Opium and opioids relieve pain. They also dull senses. And they're highly addictive.

Sigmund Freud's criticisms of religion echo Marx's.[4] Religion, for Marx and Freud, is a way of relieving, or preventing, pain.[5] It's anesthetizing and dehumanizing. Marx and Freud value pain.

Frank's criticisms of Alan's earlier religions, Christianity and television, recall Marx's and Freud's. These earlier religions might be ways for Alan to alleviate pain. This pain might include the kinship-related pain of living in the Strang home. (That might be why Dora leans on, and into, her Christianity.)

Alan's Equus-religion challenges these criticisms. It incites and involves pain. Its rituals hurt. Alan's devotion to Equus hurts, too. Its pain is excruciating.

Its pain is excruciating because its passion is electrifying. *Alan gallops.* He gallops across limits. Alan rides, ritually, toward sexual-mystical fusions. He tries to metamorphose.

And, so, he suffers. Living passionately in *Equus* comes with, and from, pain. "To go through life," Dysart tells Hesther, "and call it yours—*your life*—you first have to get your own pain" (§25/80).

Alan has done that. His pain is his. So, then, is his life.

Alan lives bound, in devotion, to Equus. Equus, for Alan and for Dysart, means passion. And this passion means pain. It means pain for Alan, and then for Dysart.

The Normal means none of them: passion, or pain, or Equus—or, really, Alan.

Dysart, following these two divinities, doubly valuates pain.[6] He devalues pain as devitalizing and destructive. And he values pain as vitalizing and vital.

But *Equus* demands that Dysart decide on one valuation, one way of valuing, in Alan's case. *Equus* insists that Dysart solve its problem: Alan's pain.

Hesther announces its solution. (From start to finish, she focuses—and refocuses Dysart and us—on Alan's pain.) "The boy's in pain," Hesther tells Dysart (§35/108). "And you," Hesther tells Dysart, "can take it away" (§35/108). That, Hesther adds, "has to be enough for you, surely? . . . In the end!" (§35/108)[7]

Maybe Hesther is persuading Dysart. Maybe she's reminding Dysart. Hesther is devoted to the Normal. So, Hesther reminds him, is Dysart. And Dysart's devotion is priestly. His devotion entails his duty.

(If Hesther is persuading Dysart, that means Dysart hasn't yet decided whether, or how, to finally act. If Hesther is reminding Dysart, she might be reminding him of a decision he's made, or a duty he's going to enact: to uncouple Equus and Alan.)

Hesther prompts the solution to Alan's pain. But Dysart has to perform it. He's the priestly problem-solver: for Alan's, and *Equus*'s, pain-problem.

That doubly conducts Alan's pain through religions. A religious devotion—Alan's, to Equus—foments Alan's pain. A religious devotion—Dysart's, to the Normal—finishes Alan's pain.

Dysart's Normal-devotion-driven act, to disjoin Alan and Equus, stops Alan's pain. It doesn't stop Dysart's. His pain comes from his passion for Alan, or from his devotion to the Normal, or from both.

Dysart begins *Equus* in pain. He ends *Equus* in pain.[8] His pain might not stop. Equus keeps calling: "Why Me?" (§35/109) (That question might be Dysart's, too.) Each call, to Dysart, is a pang.

4.4

NORMAL

IN *EQUUS*, THERE'S NO WAY around violence. Violence permeates *Equus*. *Equus* turns on violent action.

Which one(s)? That's an open question.

We might stage *Equus* in terms of violence, as a battle for Alan. At home, Dora and Frank battle. In the hospital, Hesther and Dysart battle. In the stable, Jill and Nugget and Equus battle. Throughout, Equus and the Normal battle. Alan, in different ways, ambivalently battles back.

Who wins? That depends on perspective.

Effectively, almost no one wins. Jill has a nervous breakdown. Equus loses a devotee. Nugget and five other horses are blind, or maybe dead. Dora is distraught. Frank is defeated. Alan is destroyed and ghosted. Dysart is horse-headed and haunted.

Normatively, almost everyone wins. Alan is pain-free, passion-free, sexually redirected: treated. Dora and Frank get their now-made-acceptable son back. Hesther and Dysart discharge their duties.

Either way, the Normal wins.

The Normal, Dysart tells us, "is the indispensable, murderous God of Health" (§19/62). This god is double-edged. The Normal, Dysart tells us, "both sustains and kills" (§19/62). So the Normal, Dysart tells us, "is the Ordinary made beautiful" *and* "the Average made lethal" (§19/62).

The Normal watches over *Equus*. He never appears onstage. Still, the Normal acts in *Equus*: by proxy, through others.

"I," Dysart tells us, "am his [the Normal's] priest" (§19/62). Dysart is the Normal's enactor in the long, sustaining-killing ritual of psychotherapy.[1] Through this ritual, Dysart has relieved children of terrors, agonies, and the pain they cause. Dysart has, he tells us, "cut from them parts of individuality repugnant to this God, in both his aspects" (§19/62).

Priestly Dysart follows the Normal's dogmas, however ambivalently. He performs the Normal's dictates, however reluctantly. (We might sense how ambivalently or reluctantly from how Dysart performs his Normal monologue.)

On Alan, Dysart performs a religious displacement and replacement. Dysart displaces Equus and replaces him with the Normal. Dysart replaces Alan's and Nugget's and Equus's Field of Ha Ha with, Dysart tells us, "Normal places for his [Alan's] ecstasy" (§35/109).[2]

Dysart replaces one religious reality for another. In *Equus*, there's no way out of religion.

In Normal reality, Alan is still tethered. But he's tethered to different things. Instead of Equus, Alan is tethered to the Normal. Instead of Nugget, Alan rides a scooter. Alan is bound sexually to human-human desires and interactions. For fun, he's fixed on mediatized screens.

Normal reality untethers Alan from horses and tethers him like horses. Horses are, Dysart tells us, "tethered all their lives in dim light," or "put into servitude" (§35/109). In Normal reality, that counts as proper treatment of a horse—or a human.

In both realities (Equus's and the Normal's), Alan is, differently, rendered equine. And he's subject to violence.

Whomever and whatever else *Equus* might be about, it might (also) be about the Normal and his normalizing effects. So *Equus* might perform, for us, a morality play, or a pedagogical parable: about norms, normalizations, how we divinize them, how they affect us.

A norm directs and acts and produces. It plays all these roles, as if it were staging a play. A norm enacts an aesthetic, an epistemology, an ethic. It figures who and what make sense. It figures what counts as sense, and who counts.

A norm is a way of counting. It's a metric. It's a value, and a valuing.

A norm is also a way of framing. It draws, and names, and maintains a frame. And it controls what's in the frame.

A norm regulates. It regularizes. It disciplines. It trains. It domesticates. It reins in. It makes and remakes things—like *us*.

So a norm works performatively. A norm is, performatively, power. It makes decisions and enacts them. It forms and deforms. It normalizes and abnormalizes.

Equus performs a normalization: of Alan (and, maybe, of Equus).

And us?

Where might we be in *Equus*'s Normalizing performance?

We might watch it, with and through the Normal. The Normal might be a divinized proxy for us. Or we might be humanized proxies of the Normal.

4.5

TRAGEDY

WHY DID YOU WANT *to discuss tragedy in an interview?*

Because tragedy, I think, is about questions. What we call tragedy asks questions. They're questions about us, about our limits. A tragedy questions limits we call *ours*.

How can a tragedy do that?

By crossing these limits. A tragedy performs a limit-crossing (at least one). Then it asks you about this limit-crossing.[1]

Do you think this person, in this situation, went too far, across a limit?

Do you think this person, in this situation, should have gone this far?

Do you think this person, in this situation, could have decided not to?

These questions ask you to evaluate. Then tragedy asks you to imagine.

Do you imagine you, in this situation, would (or could) have acted differently?

A tragedy double-casts you. You're you. And you're someone else.[2]

As you, a tragedy asks you to evaluate someone else's actions. It asks you to use your ways of making sense, your ways of knowing and deciding, your histories and identities and desires and relations, to evaluate.

As someone else, a tragedy asks you to imagine acting *as if* you were this other person. It asks you to make-believe your ways into this person's situation. That means make-believing your ways into this person's histories, identities, desires, relations, and ways of making sense, knowing, and deciding.

How do you think a tragedy does that?

That's a good question. It's a personal question. You're asking for my response.[3]

Are you going to respond, or are you just going to keep staring at the ceiling?

OK. I think a tragedy makes us feel *and* think, together.[4] It reminds us that we can't disconnect these acts. Interacting with a tragedy, we experience how feeling and thinking relate *for us*. That's valuable information.

And a tragedy points to some huge questions.[5] Its situated questions lead you to ask: What do you want? And what do you value? And how do you relate and enact these things? Who are you, really? And how should you live?[6] (I mean *you* singularly and plurally.)

What does that have to do with religion?

A lot, I think. What we call religion also asks us to ask questions about us. It asks us to ask these (and other) questions about us. And these questions call for decisions. With religion, we're called to act.

So tragedy and religion work together. They move us. They put us in play. Tragedy and religion expose us to ourselves, to others, to differences. They open us to questions and their uncertainties. They show us our limits. (Both are about limits.)

That all seems pretty abstract. Can you give an example from Equus?

Take Dysart's decision at *Equus*'s end. Dysart faces his dilemma: How should he treat Alan? He's pressed, from all sides, by different voices, duties, desires, divinities. Then he has to respond. Dysart has to decide, and then act.

And he does. Dysart treats Alan, with psychotherapy. Dysart destroys Alan's passion. He takes away Alan's devotion. He unbinds Alan from this devotion and binds him to another devotion: to the Normal. That'll keep Alan within Normal limits.

How, *Equus* asks us, do you evaluate Dysart's decision? If you were Dysart, *Equus* asks us to imagine, would you have made the same one? Would you have acted as Dysart does?

Are you asking me?

Well, would you?

. . . Yeah, I think so.

Why?

Because Dysart does his professional duty. Treating Alan is his job. Plus Alan's in so much pain.

So you agree with Hesther?

I guess.

And you think *Equus* is a tragedy?

Yeah.

Whose?

What do you mean?

Whose tragedy do you think *Equus* is? Who is *Equus* a tragedy for?

Alan.

How about Dysart?

Him, too.

If you have to choose between them?

That's hard.

That's tragedy.

I'm not sure how to respond.

You might consider who you think goes further across uncrossable limits. Or you might consider who you think loses more, and who *Equus* leaves more lost.

(Or you might look back at this book's terms. Each one serves as an interactive way into, or lens onto, *Equus*. You might ask "in terms of ______, whose tragedy is *Equus*?")

I don't know.

That's tragedy's point: you don't know.[7] It's not a question of knowing. It's a question of acting. And it's an open question.

Wait, do you think Equus *is a tragedy?*

Yes.

Why?

Because of what I said earlier. *Equus* does the things I think tragedy does. It exposes our vulnerabilities, our limits, our self-made limitations. The limits Alan rides across are the Normal's. The limits Dysart won't cross are the Normal's. They're the ones that frame, and fence in, what we call humanity.

Equus shows us the effects of crossing and of not crossing these limits. They're different effects—different costs. They're both high. Dysart's final monologue tells us how high.

I don't think Dysart decides to treat Alan until that monologue. I don't think Dysart's treating Alan is an inevitability, or a necessity. I think it's a painful decision. That's why, I think, Dysart delays making it as long as possible.

Dysart's decision decides things. It doesn't resolve things. I don't think *Equus* has any real resolutions, or any heroes.

Doesn't everybody think Equus *is a tragedy?*[8]

Not everybody.

What difference would that make?

Big differences, I think. If you didn't stage *Equus* in terms of tragedy, you'd have to decide on other staging terms: other directions. Plus you'd have to decide how to stage *Equus*'s last scene, especially its last lines.

We're out of time.

Thanks for the questions.

4.6

SACRIFICE

EQUUS TROUBLES OUR SENSES OF SACRIFICE.

In religion's usual terms, a sacrifice marks a bounded, ritual interaction.[1] It's ritually framed and ritually enacted. It's a performance. A sacrifice has a set, a script, and actors. One actor sacrifices a second actor for, or to, a third actor.

(Only the first actor has to be human. The second and third actors might be humans, other animals, divinities, duties, principles, relations, social or cultural formations, limits.)

This sacrificial interaction performs a transaction. A sacrifice's first actor takes something from its second actor, for its third actor. Doing so transfers its second actor across a limit—where this actor remains, wounded or wrecked (or worse). The first and third actors remain safe-and-sound. From this taking and transferring, the first actor benefits, by way of the third actor.[2]

In *Equus*, psychotherapy seems to follow this script. Psychotherapy isn't *Equus*'s only sacrifice. But it's the sacrifice *Equus* turns on.

Dysart plays the first actor. A child plays the second actor. The Normal plays the third actor. The set is Dysart's office. The psychotherapeutic process performs the sacrifice.

It's a sacerdotal performance. Dysart is a priest of the Normal. In playing this role, Dysart tells us, "I do ultimate things": "irreversible, terminal things" (§35/110). "I stand in the dark," Dysart tells us, "with a pick in my hand, striking at heads!" (§35/110) Dysart, like Alan, sacrifices those he cares for.

A psychotherapeutic sacrifice takes a long time. "Sacrifices to Zeus," Dysart tells us, "took at the most, surely, sixty seconds each" (§19/62). But "sacrifices to the Normal," Dysart tells us, "can take as long as sixty months" (§19/62). They take as long as it takes Dysart to cut from these children, he tells us, "parts of individuality repugnant to this God" (§19/62).

But psychotherapy doesn't *quite* follow sacrifice's script. Psychotherapy's first, sacrificing actor enlists its second, sacrificed actor's help. In psychotherapy, this second actor—in *Equus*, a child—isn't a passive victim. This second actor participates in his or her or their sacrifice.

That makes psychotherapy a sacrifice and a self-sacrifice. Its second actor plays two roles: in and as the sacrifice.

And it makes psychotherapy a partial sacrifice. Psychotherapy sacrifices only parts of its second actor—in *Equus*, a child. That leaves its second actor partly sacrificed. This second actor survives a partial death, as partially dead.[3]

That's how *Equus* leaves Alan. Dysart sacrifices Alan's devotional, passional, sexual equine-parts—and Alan's pain. He sacrifices the parts of Alan that the Normal demands he sacrifice.[4] Dysart sacrifices Alan by Normalizing him.[5]

Other divinities wouldn't demand this sacrifice. To other divinities—"rarer and more wonderful Gods," Dysart tells us—these sacrificed parts are "sacred" (§19/62). Dysart recognizes that.

And Dysart recognizes other divinities. He wants to tell someone, he tells Hesther, "Look! Life is only comprehensible through a thousand local Gods" (§18/58). Dysart wants to tell someone, he tells Hesther, "Worship as many as you can see—and more will appear" (§18/59).

But Dysart doesn't tell anyone, except Hesther. Dysart's psychotherapeutic sacrifices sacrifice Dysart's polytheism and pantheism.[6] They sacrifice other devotional possibilities, for an exclusive, Normal monotheism. Dysart's devotion to the Normal demands their sacrifices.

Dysart sacrifices.

Dysart sacrifices.

His sacrifices are double. Dysart is struck by the pick he uses to strike others. He slashes himself open, too.

In *Equus*, sacrifices go off-script and turn on themselves.

Alan might sacrifice Nugget to sacrifice Equus.

Alan might sacrifice Equus to save himself.

Dysart might sacrifice Equus to save Alan.

Dysart might sacrifice Alan (to the Normal) to save Alan (from Equus).

But Alan isn't saved, not really.

Neither is Dysart. By sacrificing parts of Alan, Dysart sacrifices parts of himself—knowingly or unknowingly. (Maybe Dysart sacrifices his humanity, for an interspecies half-life.)

At *Equus*'s end, Dysart is lost. He needs, he tells us, "a way of seeing in the dark" (§35/110). "What way is this?" Dysart asks us, "*What dark is this*?" (§35/110) Dysart might be left, in the dark, without a way.

We might be left in the dark, too. We're parts of *Equus*'s sacrifices. Sacrifice's tool slashes our senses or our identities, too.[7] *Equus* doesn't leave us unscathed.

4.7

ENDING

WE'VE BEEN TRACKING A MYSTERY: of *Equus*'s ending—its last lines.

Let's reset the stage for this ending.

Dysart decides, or agrees, to treat Alan. Dysart will turn his hoof-pick on Alan. He'll untie Alan and Equus. Alan won't gallop anymore. He'll be Normal. And he'll survive: partial, passionless, pain-free.

Dysart won't. He'll live through pain. He'll keep hearing *Why Me*? Untying Alan and Equus reties Equus: to Dysart. Equus won't go away.

Dysart breaks. He surrenders and confesses. "I stand in the dark," Dysart tells us, "with a pick in my hand, striking at heads!" (§35/110)

Dysart is lost. He can't see in the dark. "I cannot," Dysart tells us, "call it ordained of God: I can't get that far" (§35/110). But "I will," Dysart tells us, "pay it so much homage" (§35/110).

(Now I'm lost. Which "God"? Which "it"? This dark? This divinity? Is there a difference?)

Then Dysart delivers his last lines: "There is now, in my mouth, this sharp chain. And it never comes out" (§35/110).

How might Dysart perform these lines? How might we make sense of them?

I can't solve the mystery of *Equus*'s ending. I can see, in the dark, more ways than one: of performing, responding, making sense. I'll recount six. They make different performative ways. Some might mean recastings.

(1) Dysart's chain might not be new. It might have been there all along: chaining him to the Normal. But now, Dysart might feel this chain. He might feel himself chained. Dysart might feel when the Normal pulls on this chain. And he might sense that this chain is permanent.

That wouldn't recast Dysart. He would remain Dysart, the Normal's priest—painfully aware, now, that his child-sacrificing nightmare is his reality.

So Dysart might perform his last lines resigned. We might sense his resignation. Dysart would be lost, because Dysart would have lost.

(2) Dysart's sharp, never-coming-out chain might be made of pain. It might be an interdevotional pain. Dysart might feel himself caught between two divinities: the Normal and Equus.

Dysart might remain the Normal's priest. But that might not quell Equus's calls. Even tied to the Normal, Dysart might feel Equus's pull. And Dysart might understand that neither divinity will stop pulling.

Maybe that's why Dysart tells us "I can't get that far." Maybe, chained to the Normal, Dysart can't get as far as Equus. But he might recognize that Equus (especially now, without a devotee) demands homage.

That might shift Dysart's casting. He might now play a different Dysart: Dysart-after-Alan. This Dysart would be pained. That might be how Dysart would perform his last lines. We might sense how much pain he feels now. We might even see Dysart's mouth pulled, painfully, by an invisible chain.

(3) Dysart's chain-pain might be equine. It might be the pain a bridled horse would feel. Maybe Dysart's last words perform his interspecies horse-headedness. Maybe Dysart accepts, or embraces, this condition.

That might undo him. "The only thing I know for sure," Dysart tells us, "is this: a horse's head is finally unknowable to me" (§1/10). So horse-headed Dysart might unknow himself. He might unbecome himself. He might unbecome human—what we call, and count as, human.

That might recast Dysart as Nugget. And *Equus*'s ending might reframe *Equus*'s beginning. Dysart might, in his opening monologue, be describing himself. "What use is grief to a horse?" (§1/10) might become, for Dysart, a personal question.

Dysart might performatively signal his recasting. What if, with his last lines, Dysart put on a horse-mask? (What if he put on a horse-mask left onstage by a blinded horse-actor?)

(4) Dysart's sharp chain might represent others' pain, made his. Dysart's chain might be memory-made. Dysart might remember parts of children he sacrificed to the Normal. He might feel guilty. He might feel responsible for his Normal-sacrifices. Dysart might, finally, take responsibility for them.

That might recast Dysart as Nugget-Equus. In Alan's night-ride ritual, Nugget-Equus consumes Alan's sins. "Eat them," Alan tells his horse-divinity, "for my sake" (§21/69).

Dysart's last lines might restage this atonemental ritual. They might enact a counter-transfer of his patients' pain. Dysart might bear the burdens of their sins against the Normal. He might atone for their sins—and for his:

against his patients and other divinities. Dysart's chain might be his punishment.

(5) Dysart's chain might mean another sacrifice. It might mean another devotion. Both might be Dysart's.

Dysart realizes, and tells Alan, that Equus "won't really go that easily" (§35/108). Maybe Dysart realizes that Equus won't go at all. And Equus, without Alan, would need a new devotee.

Maybe that's Dysart. Maybe Dysart realizes that Hesther is right: he's being claimed for "a new god" (§25/82).

Dysart might realize that untying Alan from Equus requires tying himself to Equus. He might realize that his sacrificial act has to be double. Equus and the Normal both demand sacrifices.

So Dysart might sacrifice Alan to the Normal. And he might sacrifice himself to Equus. Dysart might take Alan's devotional chain, bound to Equus, and put it in his mouth. Dysart's last lines might signal his new devotion: to Equus.

Or Dysart might realize that he can untie himself from the Normal only by tying himself to Equus. Dysart might realize that he can't untie himself from all devotions. He might replace one chain with another.

Or Dysart might not realize he's being claimed by Equus. He might not realize that untying Alan from Equus would tie himself to Equus. He might not realize, until he's performed it, that his sacrifice is double. Sacrificing Alan to one divinity, Dysart might unknowingly sacrifice himself to another.

Then Dysart's devotion to Equus wouldn't be Dysart's decision. It would be Equus's. Equus might have taken Alan's devotional chain and put it in Dysart's mouth. That would satisfy Equus's devotional demand.

Dysart might perform, with his last lines, his self-sacrificed devotion to Equus. He might gaze up slightly, at Equus, looming over the spectators, as he says his last lines. These lines would performatively enact his devotion. Or he might, as he says these last lines, take a string from his pocket, and bridle himself.

(6) Dysart's last lines might mean other things. They might do other things. Dysart might perform them differently.

Maybe you've imagined other possibilities. They might be ones I haven't recounted, or haven't imagined. Either way, I want to count them.

This count could go on. *Equus*'s last lines remain (for me, at least) an open-ended mystery.[1]

4.8

VALUE

EQUUS'S ENDING LEAVES US QUESTIONING.

This book's will, too.

Questioning is critical. It's a performative way of critique. Critique names a performance-praxis. (It's a way of acting.)

Critique asks questions of value. It questions what counts as value for us. Critique questions what we value. It questions who values: who counts. And it questions how we value.[1] Critique questions ways *we* value *our* ways of valuing.

Critique's questions expose, by questioning, *us*. They show how we count who counts as *us*. Critical questions denude *us*, performatively.

They denude critique, too. Critique *is* self-critique. It's auto-critiquing.

Critique's questions can open *us*: to differences.[2] These differences might include, or make, different *whos*, different *whats*, different *hows*. They might open us to different ways of making sense, knowing, relating, judging, deciding, acting. Critique can make ways for making differences.[3]

We can't anticipate these ways or these differences. We can't prescript them. They happen, through critical, and self-critical, questioning.

These differences alter us: our values: our ways of valuing. They can make ways for revaluing.[4] Revaluing changes things. It means doing things differently.

Revaluing differences can change our frames. Values are frames and framings. They set limits. They become our limits. They make norms. So our values—who, what, how we value—make our Normal. Our values enact decisions about who and what count in these frames.

And *Equus*?

What might *Equus* value? Let's reconsider a list from an earlier scene.

Mental health? Psychotherapy? Normality? Abnormality? Imagination?

Freedom? Fidelity? Sexuality? Passion? Pain? Extremity? Worship? Divinity? Divinicide? Sacrifice? Tragedy? Transgression? Transformation?

How might this list look now? (It's the kind of list we make in Intro.) How might we revise it? What terms might we add or subtract? (It's the kind of thing we do in Intro.)

And how might *Equus* value what it values? How might *Equus* perform its values, its valuings, for us?

How might *Equus*'s performance call us to question, or into question? What differences might this performance make for us, studying religion?

How might we, studying religion, make sense of *Equus*'s case? How might *Equus*'s case make ways for us to critique, and maybe revaluate, what we call religion and how we study it?

How might you value how this book studies *Equus*'s case? How might you value, or revalue, its analyses, or its critical terms: its scene-titles? How might you critique them, and the ways they make?

What questions might you ask?

What differences might you make?

EPILOGUE

YOU MADE YOUR WAY HERE for a performance. It's happened.

Maybe it was the performance you were here for. Maybe it wasn't.

Maybe you experienced (saw, heard, thought, felt) what you expected to experience. Maybe you didn't. Maybe you experienced something unexpected.

Maybe you experienced more than one thing, at once.

That can happen with a performance. It can be and do more than one thing at once. A performance can stage multipossibilities. And it can keep them in play.

A performance can twist together enactment, criticism, critique. You can't always untwist them. That's one of performance's critical moves. It's one reason to study religion through performance.

A performance opens questions. It leaves them open. It leaves you to decide how to respond.

A performance calls for decisions. You've probably made some—even if just for now. You might change them.

You might learn something from your decisions. You might learn something about how you make them, on which (and whose) terms, in which (and whose) ways, using which (and whose) values.

Your decisions won't be final. They won't answer a performance's questions. These questions would remain: unsettled, maybe unsettling.

The performance has ended. The performance-space's lights brighten. You can see your setting, your neighbors, others. Maybe they're interacting quietly. Maybe things switch, with the lights, from hushed darkness to noisy brightness.

You're, suddenly, shot back into bodily awareness.

You move, to exit the performance-space.

What might you take away, with you, as you leave?

What differences might this performance make, for you?

Maybe as you leave, on your way somewhere else, you're already rescripting, reproducing, redirecting, reacting the performance you experienced. Maybe you're reimagining things. Maybe you're imagining different ways you might, performatively, take.

What if things were different?

ENCORE

WE BEGIN MOST MEETINGS of Intro with music. We take turns selecting songs. They can come from any time, any culture, any style. The songs relate to the play we're studying. They're songs we'd use in a particular scene if we were staging the play.

When it's my turn, with *Equus*, I usually play Patti Smith's "Land." It's on *Horses*, Patti Smith's debut album, released in 1975.[1] That makes *Equus* and *Horses* cultural contemporaries.

Maybe that's what first led me to put them together. Maybe it was their titles. Maybe it was their stories.

"Land" begins with "Horses," its first part. "Horses" begins with Patti Smith, solo, reciting a poem. A boy named Johnny, Smith says softly, was in a hallway. From the hallway's other end, she says, a rhythm generates. We hear a rhythm guitar begin to play. We hear, in the background, Smith preciting her lines. It's like a reverse echo.

Another boy slides up the hallway, merging with it. The boy looks at Johnny. Johnny wants to run. The volume and pace of "Horses" increase. Smith shifts from reciting to chanting.

The boy pushes Johnny against a locker. And, Smith chants, "he drove it in he drove it home he drove it deep in Johnny." The song's rhythm accelerates.

Then the boy disappears. Johnny falls to his knees. He starts crashing his head against a locker. He starts laughing hysterically. Smith starts to sing.

Johnny, suddenly, feels "he's being surrounded by / horses horses horses horses / coming in all directions." Johnny sees "horses horses horses / horses horses horses horses horses horses horses horses." We hear a bass guitar and percussion. Smith's chanting becomes incanting: of horses horses horses horses.

What's happening?

"Horses" begins with a scene of sexual violence between boys. That gives way to a hallucinatory, mystical vision.

It's not difficult to hear resonances of "Horses" and *Equus*. To stress them, I'd play "Horses" (in our imaginary Intro staging) during *Equus*'s final, stable scenes.

Reverberations continue as "Land" continues. Johnny rises from "his sperm coffin." He reveals knives taped to his chest. He screams, "Life is full of pain."

The I of "Land" enters the scene. I put my fingers through a horse's hair. I hand Johnny "a branch of coral flame." Waves, from a sea of possibilities, come like horses.

Johnny picks up a knife. He presses it against his throat. He lets it "dip in": to the veins, to the sea of possibilities. I feel desire's arrows. "Our lives are now entwined we will four years be together twining."

They're entwined with a horse. Johnny's nerves merge with a horse's mane. I entwine my fingers in this hair. It becomes wires through my body. Johnny feels himself disintegrate. The song plays on.

So many questions.

Why might horses be in Johnny's vision, in Smith's song?

Might Johnny's vision be religious? How might it relate to the sexual violence that precedes it?

How might horses and violence—and sex—relate in Johnny's experiences? In Alan's? What might Johnny's and Alan's equine transformations have to do with sex or violence—or religion?

Might we hear in "Land" an affective analogue of *Equus*? How might the proto-punk sounds of "Land" reverberate with the Equus noise? Could *Horses* work as *Equus*'s soundtrack, in a performance?

How might *Horses* and *Equus* relate as performance-pieces? How might they perform? How might they perform what we call religion?

What might we make of the lyrical avowal, in "Land," of "all wisdom fixed between the eyes of a horse"? What difference might it make if these eyes are (also) Johnny's?

How might the end of "Land" relate to the end of *Equus*? How might we make sense of the deaths that Johnny and Alan suffer?

Maybe Johnny does with a knife what Alan doesn't do with a hoof-pick? Maybe Johnny does with a knife what Dysart does with a hoof-pick?

Who in *Equus* might play Johnny in "Land"?

Who might play the boy?

Who might play me?

CREDITS

> One of the things I do, when I step up on a stage, when I stand up to translate, when I go to teach my classes, when I go to direct a movie, I bring everyone who has ever been kind to me with me. . . . "Everybody," I say, "come with me. I'm going on the stage. Come with me. I need you now."
>
> MAYA ANGELOU

My Intro students: for going on adventures of learning, and for prompting this book.

My Intro TAs: for sharing the pedagogical journeys, and for reassuring me so many times.

Rachel: for learning with me.

Zoran: for being my teacher for life.

Kathleen: for teaching me and teaching with me, and for opening ways of acting with joy.

Ryan: for saying the right thing at the right time, and for pointing me toward this book.

Katie: for being so invested, and for sharing a dinner that profoundly changed this book.

John, Katie, Kyle: for caring for this book, and for making it real.

Two anonymous readers: for reading this book so well, and for making it better.

Amy, Anne, Azra, Ben, Brice, Charlie, Courtney, Dan, Deb, John, Karmen, Troy: for being amazing.

Marcia and Virginia: for being lionhearts, and for playing such big parts.

Ellen and Jacob: for growing together, and for sustaining me for so long.

Michael: for working through everything, and for letting me make my way—and, then, letting go.

Biko: for sitting with me, and for recognizing cerulean blue on sight.

Mary-Jane: for making kin, and for being so wonderful.

Jon and Leah: for being my family.

Nell and Josh: for being my persons.

NOTES

1.1 MISE-EN-SCÈNE

1. Peter Shaffer, *Equus* (New York: Scribner, 2005). *Equus* has thirty-five scenes. Scenes 1–21 make up act 1. Scenes 22–35 make up act 2. In case you have a different edition, I cite *Equus* using scene numbers (marked by §), followed by page numbers from this edition. These citations appear in the text. All quotations in the text come from *Equus*.
2. "A field," Hortense Spillers writes, "finds and situates itself on its feet, on the occasions of *practice* and *performance*, inasmuch as it depends on discursive positions staked out against the apparently more settled terrain, moment by uncertain moment" (*Black, White, and in Color: Essays on American Literature and Culture* [Chicago: University of Chicago Press, 2003], x).
3. Intro situates this question, and its *we*. In Intro, *we* names fifty undergraduate students, and a teaching assistant, and me. And *we* changes every semester.
4. My reimagined Intro turns on two plays. We spend Intro's first half (five–six weeks) studying Euripides's *Bakkhai*. We spend Intro's second half (five–six weeks) studying *Equus*. Before the plays, we spend a day studying an essay by Jonathan Z. Smith. Between plays, we spend two weeks studying texts by Karl Marx, Friedrich Nietzsche, and Sigmund Freud. These texts—one essay, two plays, three pieces by the Marx-Nietzsche-Freud trio—are all we read in Intro. (Our Intro syllabus tells us that "we'll read very little. But we'll read it very, very well.") I supplement our readings with handouts. I make a one-page handout for every class meeting. These handouts collate quotations from all sorts of texts, across disciplines. Handouts' subjects follow from Intro's discussions. Students and I decide together, as we go, where our discussions will go. (Intro, even with fifty students, is a discussion class.) For more of Intro's backstory, see my "Pedagogical Cliff-Jumping," *Teaching Theology and Religion* 24, no. 1 (March 2021): 55–64.
5. Intro's approach is, according to our syllabus, of questioning and not knowing. "We'll discover," our syllabus tells us, "how *we* study religion: which paths we take, which methods we use, which terms we employ, which questions we ask, which responses we offer." And "we'll use our responses," our syllabus tells us, "to ask better questions." This approach makes our classroom, according to our syllabus, "a learning laboratory. Our class is a live, real-time experiment in learning." That means, our syllabus tells us, "all

of us are learning together." (This approach fits with my pedagogical practice. It's pretty improvisational. But improvisation requires showing up really prepared.)

6. *Equus* debuted at London's Old Vic Theatre on 26 July 1973. It was produced by the National Theatre. *Equus* opened at New York's Plymouth Theatre on 14 October 1974. It played there and then at the Helen Hayes Theatre for three years. This production won two Tony Awards, a Theatre World Award, four Outer Critics Circle Awards, and four Drama Desk Awards. Countless revivals, amateur and professional, have followed. *Equus*'s most famous revival was, probably, at London's Gielgud Theatre in 2007, and then at New York's Broadhurst Theatre in 2008, with Daniel Radcliffe playing Alan. *Equus*'s most innovative revival, I think, was at London's Theatre Royal Stratford East and then at Trafalgar Studios in 2019. It was produced by English Touring Theatre. For reviews of these productions of *Equus*, see Clive Barnes, "*Equus* a New Success on Broadway," *New York Times*, 25 October 1974; Ben Brantley, "In the Darkness of the Stable," *New York Times*, 25 September 2008; and Michael Billington, "Peter Shaffer's Homoerotic Classic Is Exhilarating," *Guardian* (US edition), 24 February 2019.
7. Peter Shaffer's plays are, Larry Bouchard writes, "tight, unified, ready to spring—even while pursuing themes of unresolved conflict that could easily split his stories apart" (*Tragic Method and Tragic Theology: Evil in Contemporary Drama and Religious Thought* [University Park: Pennsylvania State University Press, 1989], 177).
8. From *Equus*'s "first image," David Ball writes, "our curiosity is aroused; so we pay close, eager attention to things that probably held little interest for us when we entered the theatre" (*Backwards and Forwards: A Technical Manual for Reading Plays* [Carbondale: Southern Illinois University Press, 1983], 58–59).
9. I try to keep endnotes, like sentences, short. So I've invented, and followed, protocols. Each scene has no more than nine notes. Each list of texts ("on *x*, see . . .") includes no more than three. After this scene, most notes are referential, rather than expository.

1.2 IMAGINATION

1. It's a question, John Sallis writes, of "whether through imagining, through engagement with the imagined, something other can come to light" (*Force of Imagination: The Sense of the Elemental* [Bloomington: Indiana University Press, 2000], 11).
2. That involves, in John Sallis's words, "a reversal of ground and grounded, of origin and originated, of original and image—that is, of all the values, all the hierarchical oppositions, linked to the superordination of intelligible over sensible" (*Force of Imagination*, 21). Imagination, Édouard Glissant writes, "does not bear with it the coercive requirements of the idea" (*Poetics of Relation*, trans. Betsy Wing [Ann Arbor: University of Michigan Press, 1997], 192). Imagination "prefigures reality," Glissant writes, "without determining it *a priori*" (*Poetics of Relation*, 192).
3. Aesthetics refer, Kandice Chuh writes, "to the relationships among the senses and processes and structures of value-making by which certain sensibilities become common sense and others are disavowed, subjugated, or otherwise obscured" (*The Difference Aesthetics Makes: The Humanities "after Man"* [Durham, NC: Duke University Press,

2019], xii). That makes aesthetics "integral," Chuh writes, "to the production of particular kinds of difference—for example, that of the racial and colonial order, that of sex-gender regulation—as part of the naturalized visceral experience of the world" (*The Difference Aesthetics Makes*, xii).

4. A politic "consists," Jacques Rancière writes, "in reconfiguring the distribution of the sensible which defines the common of a community, to introduce into it new subjects and objects, to render visible what had not been, and to make heard those who had previously been perceived as merely noisy animals" (*Aesthetics and Its Discontents*, trans. Steven Corcoran [Malden, MA: Polity, 2009], 25).
5. "Whatever else [a] religion might be," Kathryn Lofton writes, "it is a way of describing structures by which we are bound or connected to one another" (*Consuming Religion* [Chicago: University of Chicago Press, 2017], 5). It's "also," Lofton writes, "a way of describing structures by which we distinguish ourselves from others" (*Consuming Religion*, 5). "*Religion*," Lofton writes, "is a word to intensify what we do when we name authority, practice interactions, and interpret life" (*Consuming Religion*, 13). And life includes living and dying, the living and the dead. Religion "is about," Thomas Tweed writes, "birth and natality as well as death and mortality" (*Religion: A Very Short Introduction* [Oxford: Oxford University Press, 2020], 11). "It's about," Tweed writes, "seeking joy as well as confronting suffering. It's about wonder as well as worry" (*Religion: A Very Short Introduction*, 11).
6. Aesthetic inquiry names, Kandice Chuh writes, "the procedure for calling into question the structures and processes of (e)valuation that subtend the *sensus communis* and the means by which sensibilities that differ and dissent from liberal common sense are brought to bear" (*The Difference Aesthetics Makes*, 3).

1.3 LITERATURE

1. Literature marks a space, Barbara Johnson writes, "where impasses can be kept and opened for examination" (*The Feminist Difference: Literature, Psychoanalysis, Race, and Gender* [Cambridge, MA: Harvard University Press, 1998], 13). It marks a space, Johnson writes, "where questions can be guarded and not forced into a premature validation of the available paradigms" (*The Feminist Difference*, 13). So literature names, Johnson writes, "a mode of cultural work," not "a predetermined set of works" (*The Feminist Difference*, 13).
2. "What if," Sarah Hammerschlag writes, "one could invoke a suspension of the factical without invoking the miracle?" (*Broken Tablets: Levinas, Derrida, and the Literary Afterlife of Religion* [New York: Columbia University Press, 2016], 176). And "what if," Hammerschlag writes, "all that were required was the lure of a literary text?" (*Broken Tablets*, 176).
3. "There is," Jacques Derrida writes, "no [such thing as an] essence or substance of literature" (*Demeure*, trans. Elizabeth Rottenberg [Stanford, CA: Stanford University Press, 2000], 28). "As far as literature is concerned," Rodolphe Gasché writes, "there is 'only' 'a relation called "literary"'" (*Of Minimal Things: Studies in the Notion of Relation* [Stanford, CA: Stanford University Press, 1999], 300). "Literary," Gasché writes, "rather than

being of the order of a substance or essence, is of the order of a relation" (*Of Minimal Things*, 300). Maybe that's why, Derrida writes, "the name and the thing called 'literature' remain for me, to this day, as much passions as bottomless enigmas" (*Demeure*, 20 [translation modified]).

4. Literature might name a counter-acting resistance to institutionalization. Or it might name, in Jacques Derrida's words, "a counter-institutional institution" ("'This Strange Institution Called Literature,'" trans. Geoffrey Bennington and Rachel Bowlby, in *Acts of Literature*, ed. Derek Attridge [New York: Routledge, 1992], 58). Literature would be, Derrida says, "at once institutional and wild, an institutional place in which it is in principle permissible to put in question, in any case to suspend, the whole institution" ("'This Strange Institution Called Literature,'" 58 [translation modified]). So it would be, Derrida says, "an institution which tends to overflow the institution" ("'This Strange Institution Called Literature,'" 36).

5. "Literature does not necessarily," Joseph Kronick writes, "have anything whatsoever to do with 'great books'" (*Derrida and the Future of Literature* [Albany: State University of New York Press, 1999], 10). Literature "has something to do," Kronick writes, "with performativity" (*Derrida and the Future of Literature*, 10).

6. "At stake," Kandice Chuh writes, "in the enduring question, What is literature?, is the definition of the human" (*The Difference Aesthetics Makes: The Humanities "after Man"* [Durham, NC: Duke University Press, 2019], 53). "And so," Anne Dufourmantelle writes, "this might be a good moment to speak of literature—or what goes by that name—as a figure of concerted risk-taking, that is, as an art of living" (*In Praise of Risk*, trans. Steven Miller [New York: Fordham University Press, 2019], 142).

7. "Through their very indeterminacy," Susan McHugh writes, "narrative processes thus appear to concern the very conditions of possibility for human (always along with other) ways of being" (*Animal Stories: Narrating across Species Lines* [Minneapolis: University of Minnesota Press, 2011], 2). Literature de-limits an "arena," Joseph Kronick writes, "where the relation to the other is staged" (*Derrida and the Future of Literature*, 30). "Other" names a relation. It comes, Derek Attridge writes, "in an *active* or *event-like* relation—we might prefer to call it a *relating*" (*The Singularity of Literature* [New York: Routledge, 2004], 29). This relating happens, Attridge writes, "only in the registering of that which resists my usual modes of understanding" (*The Singularity of Literature*, 27). "That moment of registering alterity," Attridge writes, "is a moment in which I simultaneously acknowledge my failure to comprehend and find my procedures for comprehension beginning to change" (*The Singularity of Literature*, 27).

8. "Religion and literature," Daniel Boscaljon and Alan Levinovitz write, "are inseparable. Religion has never existed without literature, and literature has its roots in religion" (*Teaching Religion and Literature*, ed. Daniel Boscaljon and Alan Levinovitz [New York: Routledge, 2019], 2). Their institutionalized division, Boscaljon and Levinovitz write, "grows out of tradition" (*Teaching Religion and Literature*, 2).

9. "In an age of rationalization," Hans-Thies Lehmann writes, "of the ideal of calculation and of the generalized rationality of the market, it falls to the theatre to deal with extremes of affect by means of an *aesthetics of risk*" (*Postdramatic Theatre*, trans. Karen Jürs-Munby [New York: Routledge, 2006], 186–87). These extremes become risky,

Lehmann writes, "when the spectators are confronted with the problem of having to react to what is happening in their presence" (*Postdramatic Theatre*, 187).

1.4 PERFORMANCE

1. "Performance," Diana Taylor writes, "is a practice and an epistemology, a creative doing, a methodological lens, a way of transmitting memory and identity, and a way of understanding the world" (*Performance* [Durham, NC: Duke University Press, 2016], 39). We might figure performance "in the broadest possible sense," Taylor writes, "as a process, a praxis, an episteme, a mode of transmission, an accomplishment, and a means of intervening in the world" (*Performance*, 202). "Performances," Richard Schechner writes, "mark identities, bend and remake time, adorn and reshape the body, tell stories, and allow people to play with behavior that is 'twice-behaved,' not-for-the-first-time" ("What Is Performance Studies Anyway?," in *The Ends of Performance*, ed. Peggy Phelan and Jill Lane [New York: New York University Press, 1998], 361). For other senses of performance, see Marvin Carlson, *Performance: A Critical Introduction*, 3rd ed. (New York: Routledge, 2018); Catherine Larson, "What Do We Mean When We Talk about Performance? A Metacritical Overview of an Evolving Concept," *Latin American Theatre Review* 45, no. 1 (2011): 23–44; and Philip Auslander, ed., *Performance: Critical Concepts in Literary and Cultural Studies* (New York: Routledge, 2003).
2. An act, Shoshana Felman writes, "is what *leaves traces*" (*The Scandal of the Speaking Body: Don Juan with J. L. Austin, or Seduction in Two Languages*, trans. Catherine Porter [Stanford, CA: Stanford University Press, 2002], 65).
3. "Improvisation," Jocelyn Benoist writes, "is a practice in which the irreducibility of performance comes to the fore" ("Judgment and Beyond," *Critical Inquiry* 45, no. 2 [2019]: 268). Improvisation is "not only a way of knowing," George Lewis writes, "but a way of caring, a way of attending, listening, introspecting, conducting, orienting both outward and inward, fashioning from a self a permanently permeable membrane that allows bidirectional transfer of information" ("Listening for Freedom with Arnold Davidson," *Critical Inquiry* 45, no. 2 [2019]: 440).
4. When we read, Ronald Hayman writes, "the information comes in a single jet, like water passing through a narrow hole" (*How to Read a Play* [London: Eyre Methuen, 1977], 11). But "in performance," Hayman writes, "several taps can be turned on at the same time" (*How to Read a Play*, 11).
5. "Performativity describes," Judith Butler writes, "both the processes of being acted on and the conditions and possibilities of acting" ("Rethinking Vulnerability and Resistance," in *Vulnerability in Resistance*, ed. Judith Butler, Zeynep Gambetti, and Leticia Sabsay [Durham, NC: Duke University Press, 2016], 18). Performativity can be, in José Esteban Muñoz's words, "of *or* in performance" (*Disidentifications: Queers of Color and the Performance of Politics* [Minneapolis: University of Minnesota Press, 1999], 200). "*The doing* that matters most," Muñoz writes, "and the performance that seems most crucial are nothing short of the actual making of worlds" (*Disidentifications*, 200).

6. "As an act of imagination," Diana Taylor writes, "performance allows us to imagine better scenarios and futurities" (*Performance*, 208). "Performance," José Esteban Muñoz writes, "is capable of providing a ground-level assault on a hegemonic world vision that substantiates the dominant public sphere" (*Disidentifications*, 196). So "large or small, visible or invisible," Taylor writes, "performances create change" (*Performance*, 10). A performance's point, bell hooks writes, "is to engage an audience in such a way that they not only participate but, potentially, are transformed in some way" ("Performance Practice as a Site of Opposition," in *Let's Get It On: The Politics of Black Performance*, ed. Catherine Ugwa [Seattle: Bay View Press, 1995], 218).
7. That would figure a performance, Amanda Denise Kemp writes, "both as a way of knowing and as a way of showing" ("This Black Body in Question," in *The Ends of Performance*, ed. Peggy Phelan and Jill Lane [New York: New York University Press, 1998], 116). And it would show that "embodied practice," Ben Spatz writes, "is epistemic. It is structured by and productive of knowledge" [*What a Body Can Do: Technique as Knowledge, Practice as Research* (New York: Routledge, 2015], 26).
8. On performance studies, see Shannon Jackson, "Professing Performance: Disciplinary Genealogies," *TDR* 45, no. 1 (2001): 84–95; Barbara Kirshenblatt-Gimblett, "Performance Studies," in *The Performance Studies Reader*, ed. Henry Bial and Sara Brady, 3rd ed. (New York: Routledge, 2016), 25–36; and D. Soyini Madison and Judith Hamera, "Performance Studies at the Intersections," in *The Sage Handbook of Performance Studies*, ed. D. Soyini Madison and Judith Hamera (Thousand Oaks, CA: Sage, 2006), xi–xxv. Performance studies' "ongoing challenge," Dwight Conquergood writes, "is to refuse and supersede this deeply entrenched division of labor, apartheid of knowledges, that plays out inside the academy as the difference between thinking and doing, interpreting and making, conceptualizing and creating" ("Performance Studies: Interventions and Radical Research," *TDR* 46, no. 2 [2002]: 153).
9. Performance-study "does not," Catherine Bell writes, "start out assuming what religion and ritual are" ("Performance," in *Critical Terms for Religious Studies*, ed. Mark C. Taylor [Chicago: University of Chicago Press, 1998], 211). It lets "the activities under scrutiny," Bell writes, "have ontological and analytic priority" ("Performance," 211). We then "untangle those activities," Bell writes, "in ways that can inform and modify [our] notions of religion and ritual and not simply attest to them" ("Performance," 211). On ritual as performance, see Stanley J. Tambiah, "A Performative Approach to Ritual," *Proceedings of the British Academy* 65 (1979): 113–69.

1.5 CASE

1. In case-studies, Diana Taylor writes, "the particular instances interest us only to the degree that they illuminate our larger topic" ("Double-Blind: The Torture Case," *Critical Inquiry* 33, no. 4 [2007]: 718). A case-study approach can, Taylor writes, "contribute to critical blinding" ("Double-Blind," 724).
2. "Something is deemed merely a case-study," Lauren Berlant writes, "when it doesn't

work to change the conditions of exemplarity or explanation" ("On the Case," *Critical Inquiry* 33, no. 4 [2007]: 665).

3. Case-studies are "usually," Lauren Berlant writes, "not very interesting"—and "deciders do not want them to be" ("What Does It Matter Who One Is?," *Critical Inquiry* 34, no. 1 [2007]: 1).
4. A frame, Jacques Derrida writes, "is the decisive structure of what is at stake" (*The Truth in Painting*, trans. Geoff Bennington and Ian McLeod [Chicago: University of Chicago Press, 1987], 61). No theory, no practice, no praxis "can intervene effectively," Derrida writes, "if it does not weigh up and bear on the frame" (*The Truth in Painting*, 61).
5. An event might mean, Judith Butler writes, that "we are not precisely sure what we have been through, and if we are to know in some sense what it was, that will happen in some future that we have not yet lived" ("Remarks on 'Queer Bonds,'" *GLQ* 17, nos. 2–3 [2011]: 381). On event, see Gilles Deleuze, *The Logic of Sense*, trans. Constantin V. Boundas (New York: Columbia University Press, 1990), 148–53; Jacques Derrida, "A Certain Impossible Possibility of Saying the Event," trans. Gila Walker, *Critical Inquiry* 33, no. 2 (2007): 441–61; and Erika Fischer-Lichte, "The Concept of Performance," in *The Routledge Introduction to Theatre and Performance Studies*, ed. Minou Arjomand and Ramona Masse, trans. Minou Arjomand (New York: Routledge, 2014), 41–44.
6. When a case disturbs, Lauren Berlant writes, "a personal or collective sensorium shifts" ("On the Case," 665).
7. *Equus*, Peter Shaffer says, is "not a whodunnit" (quoted in Mel Gussow, "Shaffer Details a Mind's Journey into *Equus*," *New York Times*, 24 October 1974). "Is it [*Equus*]," Gussow writes, "a whydunnit? He [Shaffer] accepted that label to a certain degree, but added, 'It's intended to be much more than that. The shadows that fall on the play are deeper'" ("Shaffer Details a Mind's Journey into *Equus*").
8. *Equus* follows Dysart, Marla Carlson writes, "as he unravels the mystery of Alan" (*Affect, Animals, and Autists: Feeling around the Edges of the Human in Performance* [Ann Arbor: University of Michigan Press, 2018], 28).

1.6 TERMS

1. "Our terms," Catherine Bell writes, "are best used as a minimalist set of props, with which we can begin to engage ideas and inquire into practices" ("Performance," in *Critical Terms for Religious Studies*, ed. Mark C. Taylor [Chicago: University of Chicago Press, 1998], 221).
2. Terms give us polythetic ways of studying religion. On polythetic approaches, see Jonathan Z. Smith, *Imagining Religion: From Babylon to Jonestown* (Chicago: University of Chicago Press, 1982), 4–5.
3. "It is the perception of incongruity," Jonathan Z. Smith writes, "that gives rise to thought" (*Map Is Not Territory: Studies in the History of Religions* [Leiden: Brill, 1978], 294). And "the most promising openings in religious studies," David Chidester writes, "can be found in critical reflection on incongruity" (*Religion: Material Dynamics* [Oak-

land: University of California Press, 2018], 5). Maybe that's because "all that we would term *religion*," Sam Gill writes, "exist[s] in the middle territory of negotiating differences, playing among incongruities" (*Storytracking: Texts, Stories, and Histories in Central Australia* [Oxford: Oxford University Press, 1998], 201).

4. "Critical terms are not critical," Catherine Bell writes, "because they contain answers" ("Performance," 220). They're critical, Bell writes, "because they point to the crucial questions at the heart of how scholars are currently experiencing their traditions of inquiry and the data they seek to encounter" ("Performance," 220). "Currently" situates these terms, these questions, these scholars, these experiences. And an "encounter" happens, Tyler Roberts writes, "when the researcher exposes his or her [or their] world, and therefore his or her [or their] questions, expectations, ideals, and analytical maps and models to the world of the religious subject, with the idea that this encounter might transform the perspective of the researcher" (*Encountering Religion: Responsibility and Criticism after Secularism* [New York: Columbia University Press, 2013], 107).
5. For three popular examples, see Mark C. Taylor, ed., *Critical Terms for Religious Studies* (Chicago: University of Chicago Press, 1998); Willi Braun and Russell T. McCutcheon, eds., *Guide to the Study of Religion* (London: Cassell, 2000); and Michael Stausberg and Steven Engler, eds., *The Oxford Handbook of the Study of Religion* (Oxford: Oxford University Press, 2016). For other lists of terms, see Carl Olson, *Religious Studies: The Key Concepts* (New York: Routledge, 2011); S. Brent Plate, ed., *Key Terms in Material Religion* (New York: Bloomsbury, 2015); and Robert A. Segal and Kocku von Stuckrad, eds., *Vocabulary for the Study of Religion* (Leiden: Brill, 2015).
6. In Intro, students generate, and curate, our critical terms. On our first day of studying *Equus*, I ask students: *What is Equus about?* Each student writes a one-word response on a slip of paper. The slips go into a bowl. A student draws a slip from the bowl and reads its word aloud. Then this student stands somewhere in our classroom. Students who support that response stand next to this student. Another student draws another slip, and the process repeats. It keeps repeating until everyone is standing. (Students can move, and keep moving, as new words are read.) Then students explain why they're standing where they're standing. Afterward, I collect the slips. They usually give us thirty-five or forty words, depending on repetitions. These words become our initial, critical terms. I put them on a handout. We add and subtract terms as we continue studying *Equus*.
7. I compiled this list from the terms in Taylor, *Critical Terms for Religious Studies*; Braun and McCutcheon, *Guide to the Study of Religion*; and Stausberg and Engler, *The Oxford Handbook of the Study of Religion*.

1.7 PROBLEMS

1. These problem-performances counter a different performance: *here's how things are*. Introductory courses often perform that. But *here's how things are* "conceal[s] from our students," in Jonathan Z. Smith's words, "the debates and uncertainties that lie behind

such judgments" (*On Teaching Religion: Essays by Jonathan Z. Smith*, ed. Christopher I. Lehrich [Oxford: Oxford University Press, 2013], 151). These judgments include what, and how, we study when we study religion. *Here's how things are* acts as if our subjects of study, Smith writes, "were self-evidently significant" (*On Teaching Religion*, 151). It treats theories as if they were facts.

2. A problem-play resists resolution, narratively or affectively. So it resists classification or containment. On problem-play, see Frederick S. Boas, *Shakespeare and His Predecessors* (London: John Murray, 1910).
3. What about psychiatry? Dysart is a psychiatrist. His perspective resembles R. D. Laing's: "to make madness, and the process of going mad, comprehensible" (*The Divided Self* [London: Penguin 2010], 9). (Shaffer's aim with *Equus* is similar: "to create a mental world in which the deed [Alan's horse-blinding] could be made comprehensible" [ix].) To do that, Laing writes, "one has to be able to orient oneself as a person in the other's scheme of things rather than only to see the other as an object in one's own world" (*The Divided Self*, 26). And "one must be able to effect this reorientation," Laing writes, "without prejudging who is right and who is wrong" (*The Divided Self*, 26). (Laing might also be describing what happens when we interact with a play.) Still, Dysart's interventions with Alan are psychotherapeutic, not psychopharmaceutic. (The one drug Dysart gives Alan, the "truth drug," is a fake.) In our contexts, psychotherapy seems better than psychiatry to describe Alan's treatment.
4. "Every play," Andrew Bennett and Nicholas Royle write, "is also about playing" (*This Thing Called Literature: Reading, Thinking, Writing* [New York: Routledge, 2015], 73). So "every play," Bennett and Royle write, "has so-called metatheatrical or metadramatic dimensions" (*This Thing Called Literature*, 73). "In other words," Bennet and Royle write, "it has things to tell us about the nature of theatre and acting" (*This Thing Called Literature*, 73). On metatheatre, see Lionel Abel, *Tragedy and Metatheatre: Essays on Dramatic Form* (New York: Holmes and Meier, 2003).
5. Peter Shaffer's "dramaturgical problems," Larry Bouchard writes, "are those of representing what by its very nature resists representation, and of dramatizing extraordinary and disturbing experiences that appear in the midst of the ordinary, the Normal" (*Tragic Method and Tragic Theology: Evil in Contemporary Drama and Religious Thought* [University Park: Pennsylvania State University Press, 1989], 188).
6. On Theatre of Cruelty, see Antonin Artaud, *The Theatre and Its Double*, trans. Mary Caroline Richards (New York: Grove, 1958), 84–104, 122–32. On Artaud's effects on Peter Shaffer's plays, see Helene L. Baldwin, "*Equus*: Theatre of Cruelty or Theatre of Sensationalism?," *West Virginia University Philosophical Papers* 25 (1979): 118–27; Gene A. Plunka, *Peter Shaffer: Roles, Rites, and Rituals in the Theatre* (Rutherford, NJ: Farleigh Dickinson University Press, 1988), 41–50; and Peter Shaffer, "The Cannibal Theatre," *Atlantic Monthly* 206 (October 1960): 48–50.
7. On Epic Theatre, see Bertold Brecht, *Brecht on Theatre: The Development of an Aesthetic*, ed. and trans. John Willett (New York: Hill and Wang, 1964), 33–42. On Brecht's effects on Peter Shaffer's plays, see Madeleine MacMurraugh-Kavanagh, *Peter Shaffer: Theatre and Drama* (London: Macmillan, 1998), 27–29; and Gene A. Plunka, *Peter Shaffer*, 37–38. "The 'Brechtian effect' of *Equus*'s staging," Ariel Watson writes, "draws the specta-

tor into complicity with the action, while also underscoring the metatheatricality of a relationship that mirrors ours (as audience) to the play: the relationship between the spectatorial therapist and the performing spectacle of the patient, whose dissection proves to be sacrificial, scientific, and almost pornographic" ("The Anxious Triangle: Modern Metatheatres of the Playwright, Actor, and Spectator" [PhD diss., Yale University, 2008], 212).

8. It might be that "the Brechtian style of the presentation," Una Chaudhuri writes, "is actually *set within* an experience much closer to the kind envisioned by Artaud" ("The Spectator in Drama/Drama in the Spectator," *Modern Drama* 27, no. 3 [1984]: 294). If so, Chaudhuri writes, "the distance, critical judgment, and rationalization implied by the lecture-hall type of seating arrangement are merely convenient ways of implicating the audience, of using its rationalistic predilections to get it to participate in what is—experientially—a secular ritual" ("The Spectator in Drama/Drama in the Spectator," 294). But "the problem is," Madeleine MacMurraugh-Kavanagh writes, "though the labels 'Brechtian' and 'Artaudian' take us some way towards an understanding of Shaffer's theatre in theoretical terms, they can never proceed beyond a certain point" (*Peter Shaffer*, 29). "It seems that Shaffer," MacMurraugh-Kavanagh writes, "has selected certain ideas from both dramatists and adapted them to create a version of theatrical drama (or dramatic theatre) that is unique to him" (*Peter Shaffer*, 29).
9. On *Equus*'s lighting, see Huai-Min Jen, "A Lighting Design for *Equus*" (MFA thesis, Texas Tech University, 1995).

1.8 QUESTION

1. In at least one earlier version of *Equus* (London: Andre Deutsch, 1973), much of this monologue appears in the last, not the first, scene of *Equus*'s second act.
2. Dysart "senses that his science," Morris Bernard Kaplan writes, "may be able to undo his [Alan's] deviant attachment; but it can neither explain nor replace the power and passion which Equus calls forth" ("*Equus*—a Psychiatrist Questions His Priestly Powers," *Hastings Center Report* 5, no. 1 [1975]: 9).
3. *Why Me*? might also ask, more broadly, how a culture or a religion gets fabricated. Why would some humans select some elements that they find in their situation, or through their imaginations? Why would they fabricate these elements into a culture, or a religion? (If these elements precede us, we can't imagine that a culture or a religion might ever be ex nihilo.)
4. A "student of religion," Jonathan Z. Smith writes, "must be relentlessly self-conscious" (*Imagining Religion: From Babylon to Jonestown* [Chicago: University of Chicago Press, 1982], xi).

2.1 STAGING

1. "In performance," Diana Taylor writes, "context is all" (*Performance* [Durham, NC: Duke University Press, 2016], 149). That's because "performance," Taylor writes, "is radically unstable, depending totally on its framing, on the *by whom* and *for whom*, on the *why where when* it comes into being" (*Performance*, 41 [my emphasis]). So a "performance cannot," Erika Fischer-Lichte writes, "be detached from its context" ("Performance as Event—Reception as Transformation," in *Theorising Performance: Greek Drama, Cultural History and Critical Practice*, ed. Edith Hall and Stephen Harrop [New York: Bloomsbury, 2013], 31). That includes bodies. "The body *is* a historical situation," Judith Butler writes, "and is a matter of doing, dramatizing, and *reproducing* a historical situation" ("Performative Acts and Gender Constitution: An Essay in Phenomenology and Feminist Theory," *Theatre Journal* 40, no. 4 [1988]: 521). On situation and standpoint, see Sandra Harding, ed., *The Feminist Standpoint Theory Reader: Intellectual and Political Controversies* (New York: Routledge, 2004).
2. This staging, Madeleine MacMurraugh-Kavanagh writes, "potentially echoes the properties of divinity which loom over the play" (*Peter Shaffer: Theatre and Drama* [London: Macmillan, 1998], 179n12).
3. On spectacting, see Augusto Boal, *Aesthetics of the Oppressed*, trans. Adrian Jackson (New York: Routledge, 2006), 86–91, 118–26. I've expanded Boal's sense, making a spectactor's involvement imaginal as well as physical.
4. Watching and being watched are relations of care. "You pay attention," Paul Woodruff writes, "because you care, and paying attention allows you to care" (*The Necessity of Theatre: The Art of Watching and Being Watched* [Oxford: Oxford University Press, 2008], 20).
5. A different staging might involve us differently. The English Touring Theatre's 2019 production would. It sat spectactors in a tiered auditorium, not onstage. Alan's horse-blinding scene ended with Alan's tearing down the curtains surrounding the stage's back and sides. Behind these curtains were powerful spotlights. As the curtains came down, the spotlights turned on. They were turned on us. We were now in the spotlights.
6. That might make us part of *Equus*'s cast. "The cast of *Equus*," Peter Shaffer writes, "sits on stage the entire evening. They get up to perform their scenes, and return when they are done to their places" (3). "They are," Shaffer writes, "witnesses, assistants—and especially a Chorus" (3).
7. Embodiments name material processes and corporeal performances. "The stylized repetition of performative acts," Erika Fischer-Lichte writes, "embodies certain cultural and historical possibilities" (*The Transformative Power of Performance: A New Aesthetics*, trans. Saskya Iris Jain [New York: Routledge, 2008], 27). "Performative acts, in turn," Fischer-Lichte writes, "generate the culturally and historically marked body as well as its identity" (*The Transformative Power of Performance*, 27). "The conditions for embodiment," Fischer-Lichte writes, "thus coincide with the conditions of performance" (*The Transformative Power of Performance*, 28). And embodiment,

Fischer-Lichte writes, "creates the possibility for the body to function as the object, subject, material, and source of symbolic construction, as well as the product of cultural inscriptions" (*The Transformative Power of Performance*, 89). Embodiment also, in Amelia Jones's words, "enacts or performs or instantiates the embodiment and intertwining of self and other" (*Body Art/Performing the Subject* [Minneapolis: University of Minnesota Press, 1998], 38). On embodiment, performance, and pedagogy, see Nathan Stucky, "Deep Embodiment: The Epistemology of Natural Performance," in *Teaching Performance Studies*, ed. Nathan Stucky and Cynthia Wimmer (Carbondale: Southern Illinois University Press, 2002), 131–44.

2.2 PERFORMANCE-TEXT

1. "You can't begin," David Ball writes, "to find [or fabricate] a play's meaning until you comprehend its works" (*Backwards and Forwards: A Technical Manual for Reading Plays* [Carbondale: Southern Illinois University Press, 1983], 3). So we should "begin," Ball writes, "by understanding its [a play's] mechanics and values" (*Backwards and Forwards*, 3).
2. "One could argue," Catherine Bell writes, "that the influence of performance terminology in religious studies has come full circle[:] from seeing action as a type of text to seeing the text as a type of activity" ("Performance," in *Critical Terms for Religious Studies*, ed. Mark C. Taylor [Chicago: University of Chicago Press, 1998], 208).
3. "It makes me think," Anne Carson writes, "of a hardboiled egg" (*Grief Lessons: Four Plays by Euripides*, trans. Anne Carson [New York: New York Review Books, 2008], 168). "Cut it open," Carson writes, and "you see an exquisite design—the yellow circle perfectly suspended within the white oval. The two shapes are disjunct and dissimilar yet construct one form. They do not contradict or cancel out, they interexist. Can you say one is prior? Circle as distorted oval? Oval as imperfect circle? Rather they each follow the other" (*Grief Lessons*, 168).
4. In genomic terms, a chiasm is where a crossing and exchange of genetic materials occur between DNA strands. On chiasm in philosophic terms, see Maurice Merleau-Ponty, *The Visible and the Invisible*, ed. Claude Lefort, trans. Alphonso Lingis (Evanston, IL: Northwestern University Press, 1968), 130–55. On reading chiasms, see Rodolphe Gasché, *Of Minimal Things: Studies in the Notion of Relation* (Stanford, CA: Stanford University Press, 1999), 263–84.
5. A supplement acts doubly. It adds to: as a surplus, from outside. And it fills in: for a lack, from inside. A supplement does both. These supplementary acts, Jacques Derrida writes, "cannot be separated" (*Of Grammatology*, trans. Gayatri Chakravorty Spivak, rev. ed. [Baltimore: Johns Hopkins University Press, 1997], 145).
6. "As soon," Jacques Derrida writes, "as the crossing goes both ways, back and forth, the same border is more or less than one" (*Aporias*, trans. Thomas Dutoit [Stanford, CA: Stanford University Press, 1993], 62 [translation modified]).
7. *Equus* might crisscross other plays, too. They might include other plays by Peter Shaf-

fer, like *The Royal Hunt of the Sun*. They might include others' plays, like Sophokles's *Oedipus Tyrannos*, or Euripides's *Hippolytos*, or maybe William Shakespeare's *Romeo and Juliet* (though I'm not sure who would play whom).

8. "A genre," Elizabeth Anker and Rita Felski write, "is not an exclusive or internally homogeneous class, but a fluid constellation of discontinuous as well as overlapping modes" (*Critique and Postcritique*, ed. Elizabeth S. Anker and Rita Felski [Durham, NC: Duke University Press, 2017], 4). "It would be hard," Michael Goldman writes, "to overestimate the extent to which drama involves the violation or testing of genre boundaries" (*On Drama: Boundaries of Genre, Borders of Self* [Ann Arbor: University of Michigan Press, 2000], 27).
9. "'Theory' and 'theatre,'" Michael Goldman writes, "derive from the same source" (*The Actor's Freedom: Toward a Theory of Drama* [New York: Viking, 1975], 113). "The theatre," Goldman writes, "is a *theatron*, a seeing place" (*The Actor's Freedom*, 113). "But the kind of seeing involved," Goldman writes, "is legitimately *theorein* as opposed to other seeing" (*The Actor's Freedom*, 113).

2.3 *INTER-*

1. "Performance studies," Richard Schechner writes, "is '*inter*'" ("What Is Performance Studies Anyway?," in *The Ends of Performance*, ed. Peggy Phelan and Jill Lane [New York: New York University Press, 1998], 360 [my emphasis]).
2. "Translation can never," Jonathan Z. Smith writes, "be fully adequate, it can never be total" (*Relating Religion: Essays in the Study of Religion* [Chicago: University of Chicago Press, 2004], 31). "Translation," Smith writes, "is necessarily incomplete" (*Relating Religion*, 31). And "this necessary incompleteness of translation means," Smith writes, "that it is corrigible" (*Relating Religion*, 31).
3. "Performing a text," Julian Hilton writes, "is an act of transmutation" (*Performance* [London: Macmillan, 1987], 4).
4. Studying performance "explores," Julian Hilton writes, "the way[s] in which the imagined, or even ineffable, becomes the real" (*Performance*, 4). "It explores," Hilton writes, "the relationship[s] between the real and representations of the real" (*Performance*, 4).
5. On interpellation, see Louis Althusser, *Lenin and Philosophy, and Other Essays*, trans. Ben Brewster (New York: Monthly Review Press, 2001), 115–24.

2.4 MASK

1. This scene casts us as psychotherapists, and Dysart as our patient. We "become," Madeleine MacMurraugh-Kavanagh writes, "analysts of the analyst" (*Peter Shaffer: Theatre and Drama* [London: Macmillan, 1998], 31). This scene becomes a psychotherapeutic session, between Dysart and us, even if the rest of *Equus* doesn't.

2. These horse-masks are, Peter Shaffer writes, "transparent: we see the actor's head through the wire head of the horse—a double image which is the preoccupation of the play" ("A Personal Essay," in *Equus*, ed. T. S. Pearce [Essex, UK: Longman, 1983], viii). On masks in *Equus*, see Susan Valeria Harris Smith, "Masks in the Modern Drama" (PhD diss., Northwestern University, 1979), 141–44. On different senses of masks, in relation to embodied differences, see Frantz Fanon, *Black Skin, White Masks*, trans. Richard Philcox (New York: Grove, 2008).
3. This ceremonial effect is "ideally," Gene Plunka writes, "similar to the [ancient] Greek ritual" (*Peter Shaffer: Roles, Rites, and Rituals in the Theatre* [Rutherford, NJ: Fairleigh Dickinson University Press, 1988], 166).
4. In *Equus*, Marla Carlson writes, "it is a human-as-horse performance onto which the audience projects its notions of animality" (*Affect, Animals, and Autists: Feeling around the Edges of the Human in Performance* [Ann Arbor: University of Michigan Press, 2018], 31).
5. "Any literalism," Peter Shaffer writes, "which could suggest the cosy familiarity of a domestic animal—or worse, a pantomime horse—should be avoided" (5). "Animal effects must be created," Shaffer writes, "through the use of legs, knees, neck, face, and the turn of the head which can move the mask above it through all the gestures of equine wariness and pride" (5).
6. They didn't in the English Touring Theatre's 2019 production. And the actors playing Jill, Frank, Dora, and Dalton also played the horse-actors.
7. On other animals in performance, see Una Chaudhuri, *The Stage Lives of Animals: Zooësis and Performance* (New York: Routledge, 2016); Lourdes Orozco, *Theatre and Animals* (London: Red Globe, 2013); and Lourdes Orozco and Jennifer Parker-Starbuck, eds., *Performing Animality: Animals in Performance Practices* (New York: Palgrave Macmillan, 2015).
8. On ancient Greek mystery religions, see Hugh Bowden, *Mystery Cults of the Ancient World* (Princeton, NJ: Princeton University Press, 2010); and Walter Burkert, *Ancient Mystery Cults* (Cambridge, MA: Harvard University Press, 1989). We might read *Equus* in relation to Dionysos. (We do in Intro, reading *Equus* with *Bakkhai*.) I mean Dionysos, the ancient Greek divinity of mask, drama, tragedy, intoxication, transformation. I don't mean the Dionysian. On *Equus* in terms of Apollonian-Dionysian dynamics, see Madeleine MacMurraugh-Kavanagh, *Peter Shaffer*, 103–15; and Doyle W. Walls, "*Equus*: Shaffer, Nietzsche, and the Neuroses of Health," *Modern Drama* 27, no. 3 (1984): 314–23. But *Equus* refigures these dynamics "in such a comprehensive way," I. Dean Ebner writes, "as to put on the stage at once nearly everything over which we struggle" ("The Double Crisis of Sexuality and Worship in Shaffer's *Equus*," *Christianity and Literature* 31, no. 2 [1982]: 29).
9. See Karl Marx, "Toward a Critique of Hegel's *Philosophy of Right*: Introduction," trans. Loyd D. Easton and Kurt H. Guddat, in *Selected Writings*, ed. Lawrence Simon (Indianapolis: Hackett, 1994), 28; Friedrich Nietzsche, *The Gay Science*, ed. Bernard Williams, trans. Josefine Nauckhoff (Cambridge: Cambridge University Press, 2001), §125, 120; and Sigmund Freud, *The Future of an Illusion*, trans. J. A. Underwood (London: Penguin, 2008).

2.5 PLAY

1. "Play," David Miller writes, "becomes the root metaphor of the study of religion under the conditions of the death of God" (*Gods and Games: Toward a Theology of Play* [New York: Harper and Row, 1973], xxix). And "the 'logic' of play," Miller writes, "is the 'logic' of '*as if*'" (*Gods and Games*, 20 [my emphasis]).
2. "Play designates," Sam Gill writes, "the vitality, the movement that arises in differences" (*Dancing Culture Religion* [Lanham, MD: Lexington Books, 2012], 147). On play as moving differences, see Jacques Derrida, *Writing and Difference*, trans. Alan Bass (Chicago: University of Chicago Press, 1978), 278–93.
3. On safe-and-sound, see Jacques Derrida, "Faith and Knowledge: The Two Sources of 'Religion' at the Limits of Reason Alone," trans. Samuel Weber, in *Religion*, ed. Jacques Derrida and Gianni Vattimo (Stanford, CA: Stanford University Press, 1998), 1–78. Derrida counts the safe-and-sound (aka the sacred or the unscathed) as one of religion's two sources.
4. Play makes, Richard Schechner writes, "its own (permeable) boundaries and realms: multiple realities that are slippery, porous" (*The Future of Ritual: Writings on Culture and Performance* [New York: Routledge, 1993], 26).
5. "Play," Sam Gill writes, "is möbiatic in this sense: the inside and outside are so seamlessly connected as to be self-problematizing" ("Play," in *Guide to the Study of Religion*, ed. Willi Braun and Russell T. McCutcheon [London: Cassell, 2000], 454). "In play, the realms we otherwise carefully keep separate," Eugen Fink writes, "are mixed and blended" (*Play as Symbol of the World*, trans. Ian Alexander Moore and Christopher Turner [Bloomington: Indiana University Press, 2016], 208). Play happens, Gill writes, "where there is an appreciation of the importance of interactivity, interdependence, interplay to gain a deep sophisticated understanding of anything" ("Play as Pedagogy," unpublished manuscript [http://sam-gill.com/PDF/Play%20and%20Pedagogy.pdf], 3).
6. Play, Thomas Henricks writes, "does not narrow but rather opens up possibility" (*Play and the Human Condition* [Urbana: University of Illinois Press, 2015], 37). So play "will not," Eugen Fink writes, "lead us out of the labyrinth of questions, but deeper into them" (*Play as Symbol of the World*, 70). "Play," Miguel Sicart writes, "reambiguates the world" (*Play Matters* [Cambridge, MA: MIT Press, 2014], 28).
7. "It's Dysart's task," Madeleine MacMurraugh-Kavanagh writes, "to murder Alan's replacement deity and return Alan to the 'normal world'" (*Peter Shaffer: Theatre and Drama* [London: Macmillan, 1998], 95).
8. "Play is fundamentally," Thomas Henricks writes, "a sense-making activity" (*Play and the Human Condition*, 209). But for play's sense-making, Eugen Fink writes, "the appropriate categories do not easily and unambiguously present themselves" (*Play as Symbol of the World*, 26).
9. In play, we learn, Sam Gill writes, "to make choices, to reflect on the process of making choices, and to question our understanding of how choices are made" ("Play," 454). And "choice depends," Gill writes, "upon a hierarchy of values" ("Play," 454).

2.6 ACTING

1. This question is also Dysart's (§22/74). It's the question prompted by *Why Me*?
2. "The fundamental principle of religion," Erika Fischer-Lichte writes, "is action" (*Theatre, Sacrifice, Ritual: Exploring Forms of Political Theatre* [New York: Routledge, 2005], 31). Acting matters for religion, and for studying religion, because religion and studying religion shuttle between, or straddle, or crisscross acting's two senses.
3. "Play," Eugen Fink writes, "is an exhilarated 'doing *as if*'" (*Play as Symbol of the World*, trans. Ian Alexander Moore and Christopher Turner [Bloomington: Indiana University Press, 2016], 54 [my emphasis]).
4. *As if*, Jacques Derrida writes, "plays a decisive role in the coherent organization of our experience[s]" (*Without Alibi*, ed. and trans. Peggy Kamuf [Stanford, CA: Stanford University Press, 2002], 211). And "does not a certain '*as if*,'" Derrida asks, "mark, in thousands of ways, the structure and the mode of being of all objects belonging to the academic field[s] called the humanities, whether they be the humanities of yesterday or today or tomorrow?" (*Without Alibi*, 212 [my emphasis])
5. An ethic, Judith Butler writes, "requires us to risk ourselves precisely at moments of unknowingness, when what forms us diverges from what lies before us" (*Giving an Account of Oneself* [New York: Fordham University Press, 2005], 136). They're moments when our undoing is, Butler writes, "a chance—to be addressed, claimed, bound to what is not me, but also to be moved, to be prompted to act, to address myself elsewhere" (*Giving an Account of Oneself*, 136).
6. For a virtue ethic, see Aristotle, *Nicomachean Ethics*, trans. Joe Sachs (Newburyport, MA: Focus, 2002). For a duty ethic, see Immanuel Kant, *Groundwork of the Metaphysics of Morals*, ed. and trans. Mary Gregor and Jens Timmermann, rev. ed. (Cambridge: Cambridge University Press, 2012). For a utilitarian ethic, see John Stuart Mill, *Utilitarianism*, ed. George Sher, 2nd ed. (Indianapolis: Hackett, 2001). For a care ethic, see Nel Noddings, *Caring: A Relational Approach to Ethics and Moral Education*, 2nd ed. (Berkeley: University of California Press, 2013). For a responsibility ethic, see Emmanuel Levinas, *Otherwise Than Being, or Beyond Essence*, trans. Alphonso Lingis (Pittsburgh: Duquesne University Press, 1998). There are other sorts, and traditions, of ethics. I've cited one example of each of these five sorts, from Euro-American traditions. (Maybe you can supplement this list. I hope so.) For a critique of these ethical traditions, see Friedrich Nietzsche, *On the Genealogy of Morality*, ed. Keith Ansell-Pearson, trans. Carol Diethe, 3rd ed. (Cambridge: Cambridge University Press, 2017).
7. "The instant of decision, the one in which a risk is taken," Anne Dufourmantelle writes, "inaugurates an *other* time, much as trauma does. But a positive trauma" (*In Praise of Risk*, trans. Steven Miller [New York: Fordham University Press, 2019], 2). And "if risk is the event of 'not dying,'" Dufourmantelle writes, it's "a physical engagement at close quarters with the unknown" (*In Praise of Risk*, 7). "It thus opens," Dufourmantelle writes, "the possibility that something unhoped for will happen" (*In Praise of Risk*, 7).
8. *Equus*, Thomas Akstens writes, "is Dysart's play, and he does what we demand that he do" ("Redression as a Structural Imperative in Shaffer's *Equus*," *Journal of Dramatic*

Theory and Criticism 6, no. 2 [1992]: 97). "Dysart," Peter Shaffer writes, "has to do what he does" ("A Personal Essay," in *Equus*, ed. T. S. Pearce [Essex, UK: Longman, 1983], ix). But does he, really?

9. "Tragedy," Peter Shaffer writes, "does not lie in a conflict of Right and Wrong, but in a collision between two [or more] different kinds of Right" ("A Personal Essay," ix).

2.7 MAKE-BELIEVE

1. Literature's appeal to us is, in Jacques Derrida's words, "*you have to believe me because you have to believe me*" (*Demeure*, trans. Elizabeth Rottenberg [Stanford, CA: Stanford University Press, 2000], 40 [translation modified, my emphasis]).
2. On belief and credit, see Jacques Derrida, "Faith and Knowledge: The Two Sources of 'Religion' at the Limits of Reason Alone," trans. Samuel Weber, in *Religion*, ed. Jacques Derrida and Gianni Vattimo (Stanford, CA: Stanford University Press, 1998), 1–78. By Derrida's count, belief and credit are, together, one of religion's two sources.
3. *As if* is, Colby Dickinson writes, "the lynchpin of belief" (*Words Fail: Theology, Poetry, and the Challenge of Representation* [New York: Fordham University Press, 2017], 11). *As if* is "the paradoxical (aporetic) essence," Dickinson writes, "of what constitutes any attempt to formulate belief" (*Words Fail*, 14).
4. *Some other* invokes, and translates, part of a phrase of Michel de Certeau's: "*un rapport à* de l'autre" ("What We Do When We Believe," trans. Richard Miller, in *On Signs*, ed. Marshall Blonsky [Baltimore: Johns Hopkins University Press, 1985], 192). What might this "de l'autre" mean? Another? An other? Any other? Someone other? Some otherness? Maybe something else?
5. Believing is "a modality," Michel de Certeau writes, "of the affirmation, not its content" (*The Practice of Everyday Life*, trans. Steven Rendall [Berkeley: University of California Press, 1984], 178 [translation modified]).
6. "Relation struggles," Édouard Glissant writes, "and states itself in opacity. It defers self-importance" (*Poetics of Relation*, trans. Betsy Wing [Ann Arbor: University of Michigan Press, 1997], 186). It's, Glissant writes, "the knowledge in motion of beings, which risks the being of the world" (*Poetics of Relation*, 187).
7. On what we call reality, in relation to sciences and their stories, see Karen Barad, *Meeting the Universe Halfway: Quantum Physics and the Entanglement of Matter and Meaning* (Durham, NC: Duke University Press, 2007); Lynn Margulis and Dorion Sagan, *What Is Life?* (Berkeley: University of California Press, 2000); and Mary-Jane Rubenstein, *Worlds without End: The Many Lives of the Multiverse* (New York: Columbia University Press, 2014).
8. "The power of make-believe," Michael Taussig writes, "is essential to religious force" ("Transgression," in *Critical Terms for Religious Studies*, ed. Mark C. Taylor [Chicago: University of Chicago Press, 1998], 356). Without this power, Taussig writes, "there can be no religion" ("Transgression," 356).

2.8 PLAY-IN-PLAY

1. On Dysart's addresses to us, see Katherine A. Hogan, "Talking to the Audience: Narrative Characters in Twentieth-Century Drama" (PhD diss., St. John's University, 2005), 73–86.
2. "There is," Michael Goldman writes, "always a play-within-the-play" (*The Actor's Freedom: Toward a Theory of Drama* [New York: Viking, 1975], 16). The realities we discover there allow us, Goldman writes, "at once an escape from self and a confrontation of self" (*The Actor's Freedom*, 110). A play is, in Barbara Freeman's words, "a culturally conditioned mode of staging the construction of the real" (*Staging the Gaze: Postmodernism, Psychoanalysis, and Shakespearean Comedy* [Ithaca, NY: Cornell University Press, 1991], 50).
3. Testimony always presents, Jacques Derrida writes, "at least the *possibility* of fiction" (*Demeure*, trans. Elizabeth Rottenberg [Stanford, CA: Stanford University Press, 2000], 27). Testimony appeals to, Derrida writes, "a certain system of belief, of belief without proof" (*Demeure*, 49). And "a novel, a poem, or a play," J. Hillis Miller writes, "is a kind of testimony. It bears witness" (*On Literature* [New York: Routledge, 2002], 39). Testimony also presents at least the possibility of lying. On lying, see Jacques Derrida, *Without Alibi*, ed. and trans. Peggy Kamuf (Stanford, CA: Stanford University Press, 2002), 28–70.
4. "Critique emerges," Amy Hollywood writes, "as a self-conscious modality in those moments when we realize that we occupy the world differently—or desire to occupy the world differently—than at least some part of the traditions into which we have been born demand" (*Acute Melancholia, and Other Essays: Mysticism, History, and the Study of Religion* [New York: Columbia University Press, 2016], 17.

3.1 CASTING

1. "Theatre is fundamentally concerned," Colette Conroy writes, "with the human body" (*Theatre and the Body* [New York: Palgrave Macmillan, 2010], 8). "The body," Jean-Luc Nancy writes, "is that which comes, approaches a stage" ("Body—Theatre," in *Expectation: Philosophy, Literature*, trans. Robert Bononno [New York: Fordham University Press, 2018], 156). "And the theatre," Nancy writes, "is that which gives place to a body's approach" ("Body—Theatre," 156 [translation modified]). Theatre "allows us to ask," Conroy writes, "what we mean when we talk about bodies" (*Theatre and the Body*, 8). We might mean "that the body," Judith Butler writes, "despite its clear boundaries, or perhaps by virtue of those very boundaries, is defined by the relations that make its own life and action possible" ("Rethinking Vulnerability and Resistance," in *Vulnerability in Resistance*, ed. Judith Butler, Zeynep Gambetti, and Leticia Sabsay [Durham, NC: Duke University Press, 2016], 16). And "when you point at a body," Conroy writes, "you must always point at a specific body in a specific place, and the complexity of the body means

that you are pointing at a complex system, not at an object" (*Theatre and the Body*, 16). "To understand the ontological complexity of the actor's body," David Graver writes, "we need to look not for two forms of existence there [character and performer] but (at least) seven" ("The Actor's Bodies," *Text and Performance Quarterly* 17, no. 3 [1997]: 222). These embodied forms are, Graver writes, "characters, performers, commentators, personages, members of socio-historical groups, physical flesh, and loci of private sensations" ("The Actor's Bodies," 222).

2. "Questions about what sorts of bodies," Colette Conroy writes, "may appear on stage, questions about who may play which part, are important to the way we understand and make theatre" (*Theatre and the Body*, 4). On thinking through some of these questions and decisions, in different ways, see Dorinne Kondo, *Worldmaking: Race, Performance, and the Work of Creativity* (Durham, NC: Duke University Press, 2018); Angela C. Pao, *No Safe Spaces: Re-casting Race, Ethnicity, and Nationality in American Theatre* (Ann Arbor: University of Michigan Press, 2010); and Carrie Sandahl and Philip Auslander, eds., *Bodies in Commotion: Disability and Performance* (Ann Arbor: University of Michigan Press, 2005).
3. These questions involve critical practices. And these practices involve, Amelia Jones writes, "the *making visible* of whiteness: the 'outing' of whiteness" ("Whiteness," in *Reading Contemporary Performance: Theatricality across Genres*, ed. Meiling Cheng and Gabrielle H. Cody [New York: Routledge, 2016], 279). Doing so "exposes," Jones writes, "the ideological force of its [whiteness's] privileges, denaturalizing its 'invisible' but ubiquitous claim to power" ("Whiteness," 279).
4. They did in the English Touring Theatre's 2019 production of *Equus*.

3.2 RELATIONS

1. I'm performing this sentence-couple as I write this sentence. I'm doing so even though I'm writing it at home—where I've been for months (without leaving), by myself, in quarantine. It's because I'm exposed, and I'm not alone, that I'm in quarantine.
2. "Thinking is," Mary-Jane Rubenstein writes, "the continually renewed and, for the most part, continually failed attempt to expose itself to exposure itself, when exposure is only itself in relation" (*Strange Wonder: The Closure of Metaphysics and the Opening of Awe* [New York: Columbia University Press, 2008], 115). On relation, see Ashon T. Crawley, *The Lonely Letters* (Durham, NC: Duke University Press, 2020); Donna J. Haraway, *Staying with the Trouble: Making Kin in the Chthulucene* (Durham, NC: Duke University Press, 2016); and Jean-Luc Nancy, *Being Singular Plural*, trans. Robert D. Richardson and Anne E. O'Byrne (Stanford, CA: Stanford University Press, 2000).
3. In Intro, we perform *Equus*'s relations and their effects in *tableaux vivants*. Students divide into groups of five or six. Within each group, they decide which of *Equus*'s players they'll be. Then they use their bodies interactively, to arrange their group's *tableau vivant*. Their bodily relations depict how they make sense of *Equus*'s relations and their effects on players. Heads, hands, arms, and legs usually come into play. So, sometimes,

do feet, ankles, elbows, necks, backs, and bottoms. Often, students use their clothing, too. For example, I've seen scarves used as handcuffs, or as blindfolds, or as bridles. Once a group is positioned, other groups try to figure out who's who, and how they relate to each other, and how their relations affect each other. (These things aren't, ideally, immediately obvious.)

4. Family "endures," Kathryn Lofton writes, "as the story within every story" (*Consuming Religion* [Chicago: University of Chicago Press, 2017], 284). And "family relations are," David Ball writes, "at or near the center of almost every play" (*Backwards and Forwards: A Technical Manual for Reading Plays* [Carbondale: Southern Illinois University Press, 1983], 85). "Don't ignore this superb means," Ball writes, "for understanding the play and bringing audiences close to it" (*Backwards and Forwards*, 85).
5. "The origin of religion is," Kathryn Lofton writes, "the asking of questions about who kin are and what keeps them as such" (*Consuming Religion*, 175). And "kinship," Lofton writes, "is a bigger category [than family]" (*Consuming Religion*, 184). "The family is," Judith Butler says, "but one historical instance of kinship" ("Disruptive Kinship," in the discussion "Affinities: Villa Gillet's Walls and Bridges Series," with Hélène Cixous and Avital Ronell, New School, 24 October 2011 [video, 1:49:18; https://youtu.be/8k91WwJIhl8]). Kinship names, Elizabeth Freeman writes, "a set of acts that may or may not follow the officially recognized lines of alliance and descent" ("Queer Belongings," in *A Companion to Lesbian, Gay, Bisexual, Transgender, and Queer Studies*, ed. George C. Haggerty and Molly McGarry [Malden, MA: Blackwell, 2007], 305).
6. "Conceiving of alternative structures of collectivity," Kathryn Lofton writes, "requires not that we eradicate human desire but that we imagine new ways to share what we have and care for with those who have not" (*Consuming Religion*, 288). "There is," Lofton writes, "nothing easy about this work. It requires reimagining our every move and reconceiving every border" (*Consuming Religion*, 288). That's humanities' work. "The role of the humanities must be," Kandice Chuh writes, "to amplify relationality in an effort to delegitimize and defunction the rationalism that so affirmatively justifies unlivability" (*The Difference Aesthetics Makes: The Humanities "after Man"* [Durham, NC: Duke University Press, 2019], 95). "This is," Chuh writes, "both a simple and difficult project" (*The Difference Aesthetics Makes*, 95).
7. These relations would be queerly corporeal. "As a practice," Elizabeth Freeman writes, "kinship is resolutely corporeal" ("Queer Belongings," 298). "Kinship 'matters,'" Freeman writes, "in the way that bodies 'matter'" ("Queer Belongings," 298). And "if kinship is anything at all," Freeman writes, it's "a set of representational and practical strategies for accommodating all the possible ways one human being's body can be vulnerable and hence dependent upon that of another, and for mobilizing all the possible resources one body has for taking care of another" ("Queer Belongings," 298).
8. "Kinship," Judith Butler says, "is the mode of living out a set of passions that constantly disrupt one another" ("Disruptive Kinship").

3.3 IMAGE

1. "This image [of Christ]," Dora tells Dysart, "certainly would not have been my choice, but I don't believe in interfering too much with children, so I said nothing" (§11/39).
2. "God is dead!" Friedrich Nietzsche writes: "And we have killed him!" (*The Gay Science*, ed. Bernard Williams, trans. Josefine Nauckhoff [Cambridge: Cambridge University Press, 2001], §125, 120). "The holiest and the mightiest thing," Nietzsche writes, "the world has ever possessed has bled to death under our knives" (*The Gay Science*, §125, 120).
3. Madeleine MacMurraugh-Kavanagh also names Equus as "Alan's replacement deity" (*Peter Shaffer: Theatre and Drama* [London: Macmillan, 1998], 95).
4. On comparison in studying religion, see Aaron W. Hughes, *Comparison: A Critical Primer* (Sheffield, UK: Equinox, 2017); Luther H. Martin, "Comparison," in *Guide to the Study of Religion*, ed. Willi Braun and Russell T. McCutcheon (London: Cassell, 2000), 45–56; and Kimberley C. Patton and Benjamin C. Ray, eds., *A Magic Still Dwells: Comparative Religion in the Postmodern Age* (Berkeley: University of California Press, 2000).
5. "The notion of the god who is, because a god, then everywhere," Patrick Hutchings writes, "is not an aside in the play [*Equus*]" ("*Equus* and the Concept of Worship," *Sophia* 33, no. 1 [1994]: 27). "It lies," Hutchings writes, "as all the images of seeing and blinding show, at the center of the play's action" ("*Equus* and the Concept of Worship," 27).
6. On seeing, see John Berger, *Ways of Seeing* (New York: Penguin, 1977); and Robert S. Nelson, "Vision," in *Key Terms in Material Religion*, ed. S. Brent Plate (New York: Bloomsbury, 2015), 267–74.
7. "Theatre is the art," Paul Woodruff writes, "of finding human action worth watching" (*The Necessity of Theatre: The Art of Watching and Being Watched* [Oxford: Oxford University Press, 2008], 22). And "part of our need to watch theatre," Woodruff writes, "grows from our need to care about other people" (*The Necessity of Theatre*, 20). "Theatre is most theatre," Woodruff writes, "when the arts of watching and being watched merge and give way to shared action, shared experience, a shared moment of transcendence" (*The Necessity of Theatre*, 229).

3.4 HUMAN-HORSE-DIVINITY

1. "When *Equus* was first produced," Larry Bouchard writes, "and for a long time thereafter, there was little consensus as to what it was about" (*Tragic Method and Tragic Theology: Evil in Contemporary Drama and Religious Thought* [University Park: Pennsylvania State University Press, 1989], 188).
2. "Human-horse co-existence," Natalie Corinne Hansen writes, "dates back 5500 years before the present to the Botai people," in present-day Kazakhstan ("Horse Stories: Rethinking the Human-Animal Divide" [PhD diss., University of California, Santa Cruz, 2009], 5). Horses are "a species that is unique within the animal kingdom," Kristen Guest and Monica Mattfeld write, "in its relationship and interdependence with

humans" (*Equestrian Cultures: Horses, Human Society, and the Discourse of Modernity*, ed. Kristen Guest and Monica Mattfeld [Chicago: University of Chicago Press, 2019], 1). A horse, Vinciane Despret writes, "*embodied* the chance to explore other ways by which human and non-human bodies become more sensitive to each other" ("The Body We Care For: Figures of Anthropo-zoo-genesis," *Body and Society* 10, nos. 2–3 [2004]: 114). For example, "talented riders," Despret writes, "behave and move like horses" ("The Body We Care For," 115). These riders' "human bodies," Despret writes, "have been transformed by and into a horse's body" ("The Body We Care For," 115).

3. "Without the horse," Elaine Walker writes, "humans would be different" (*Horse* [London: Reaktion Books, 2008], 12). So would humans', and others', histories. "At whatever level we relate to the horse," Walker writes, "it is so closely linked with human development that without it our own history would be completely different" (*Horse*, 12). "The horse is written," Walker writes, "so intrinsically into our human history that attempting to identify key aspects of its role becomes an exercise in leaving out rather than including" (*Horse*, 193).
4. On human-horse relations in performance, see Una Chaudhuri, *The Stage Lives of Animals: Zooësis and Performance* (New York: Routledge, 2016), 181–95; Kim Marra, "Horseback Views: A Queer Hippological Performance," in *Animal Acts: Performing Species Today*, ed. Una Chaudhuri and Holly Hughes (Ann Arbor: University of Michigan Press, 2014), 111–40; and Lourdes Orozco and Jennifer Parker-Starbuck, eds., *Performing Animality: Animals in Performance Practices* (New York: Palgrave Macmillan, 2015). On horses' roles in *Equus*, see Kimberly Poppiti, "Pure Air and Fire: Horses and Dramatic Representations of the Horse on the American Theatrical Stage" (PhD diss., New York University, 2003), 210–25.
5. It might, in Kristen Guest and Monica Mattfeld's words, "complicate formulations of identity and otherness central to our historical understanding of human-animal relationship[s]" (*Equestrian Cultures*, 2). Thinking historically, "the horses in *Equus*," Marla Carlson writes, "typify British horses in the second half of the twentieth century" (*Affects, Animals, and Autists: Feeling around the Edges of the Human in Performance* [Ann Arbor: University of Michigan Press, 2018], 30).
6. The hybrids Dysart mentions are centaurs. Centaurs mix a human torso and an equine body. In ancient Greek religions, they "were fathered," Elaine Walker writes, "by the monster Centaurus upon the mares of Pelion" (*Horse*, 51). And they "were linked," Walker writes, "to the wild revelry associated with Dionysos" (*Horse*, 51). On centaurs in *Equus*, see Melanie Kage, "Of Men and Centaurs: Identity and the Relationship of Humans and Horses in Peter Shaffer's *Equus*" (MA thesis, Linköping University, 2010).
7. Alan might also (or instead) morph into Christ. Alan "becomes the Christ figure," Leonard Mustazza writes, "as he reinterprets and plays out Christ's passion, replete with actual corporeal punishment" ("A Jealous God: Ritual and Judgment in Shaffer's *Equus*," *Papers on Language and Literature* 28, no. 2 [1992]: 178).
8. "Equine labor has become affective," Marla Carlson writes, so that "if *Equus* were written today, perhaps it would be a horse providing therapy to Alan Strang after he blinded six men" (*Affect, Animals, and Autists*, 30–31).
9. In a performance, this line might sound like "I'm wearing that horse's head: myself."

And "wearing that horse's head" would make Dysart an inverted centaur, with a horse's head and a human body.

3.5 DEVOTION

1. On worship in *Equus*, see Patrick Hutchings, "*Equus* and the Concept of Worship," *Sophia* 33, no. 1 (1994): 14–31; Barbara Lounsberry, "'God-Hunting': The Chaos of Worship in Peter Shaffer's *Equus* and *The Royal Hunt of the Sun*," *Modern Drama* 21, no. 1 (1978): 13–28; and James R. Stacy, "The Sun and the Horse: Peter Shaffer's Search for Worship," *Educational Theatre Journal* 28, no. 3 (1976): 325–37.
2. This question, in *Equus*, relates to questions of sexuality. In *Equus* "there is no successful transition," Neil Timm writes, "to heterosexual fulfillment that includes worship" ("*Equus* as a Modern Tragedy," *Philological Papers* 25 [1979]: 129).
3. "If the performative," Shoshana Felman writes, "is an event—a ritual—of desire, should we be surprised to learn that performative desire always takes as its model, rhetorically, the symbolics of sexual desire?" (*The Scandal of the Speaking Body: Don Juan with J. L. Austin, or Seduction in Two Languages*, trans. Catherine Porter [Stanford, CA: Stanford University Press, 2002], 76).

3.6 SEXUALITY

1. "Sexuality," Michel Foucault writes, "must not be conceived of as a given sort of nature that power would try to subdue, or as an obscure domain that knowledge would attempt, little by little, to unveil" (*History of Sexuality*, vol. 1, trans Robert Hurley [New York: Vintage, 1990], 105 [translation modified]).
2. "What if," Judith Butler writes, "sexuality is the means by which I am dispossessed? What if it is invested and animated from elsewhere even as it is precisely mine?" (*Undoing Gender* [New York: Routledge, 2004], 16). Wouldn't that mean, Butler writes, "that the 'I' who would 'have' its sexuality is undone by the sexuality it claims to have" (*Undoing Gender*, 16)?
3. Sexuality names "a historical apparatus," Michel Foucault writes: "a large surface network in which the stimulation of bodies, the intensification of pleasures, the incitement to discourse, the formation of knowledges, the reenforcement of controls and resistances, are linked together" (*History of Sexuality*, vol. 1, 105–6 [translation modified]). On sexuality's terms, see Jeffrey Weeks, *The Languages of Sexuality* (New York: Routledge, 2011).
4. "Thinking of sex *with* animals," Vinciane Despret writes, "is a test of the evidences and norms that guide our ways of thinking" (*What Would Animals Say If We Asked the Right Questions?*, trans. Brett Buchanan [Minneapolis: University of Minnesota Press, 2016], 205).

5. "Sexuality is a fissure," Michel Foucault writes, "that traces the limit in us and designates us as ourselves a limit" ("A Preface to Transgression," trans. Donald F. Bouchard and Sherry Simon, in *Aesthetics, Epistemology and Method*, ed. James D. Faubion [New York: New Press, 1998], 70 [translation modified]).
6. "At the heart," C. J. Gianakaris writes, "of their [Dora and Frank's] differences are matters of religion and sex" (*Peter Shaffer* [London: Macmillan, 1992], 95). Dora contains sexuality within a religion. Frank makes sexuality into a religion.
7. *Equus* "is a play," T. S. Pearce writes, "about Martin Dysart and Alan Strang" (Pearce, introduction to *Equus*, ed. T. S. Pearce [Essex, UK: Longman, 1983], xi). "But if you want to give it [*Equus*] an abstract subject," Pearce writes, "then it is a play about religion and sex, or sex and religion, according to where you place the greater emphasis" (*Equus*, xi). And we "may view," James Stacy writes, "the interrelation of sex and religion as an historical fact" ("The Sun and the Horse: Peter Shaffer's Search for Worship," *Educational Theatre Journal* 28, no. 3 [1976]: 332).
8. "When Alan begins," Gene Plunka writes, "to identify with Equus, the horse-god, the relationship becomes sexual" (*Peter Shaffer: Roles, Rites, and Rituals in the Theatre* [Rutherford, NJ: Farleigh Dickinson University Press, 1988], 158).
9. Alan's screaming and trumpeting are interreligious acts. They also recall the Strangs' familial, religious-sexual entanglements, through stories Dora tells Alan. "Did you know," Dora asks Alan, "that when Christian cavalry first appeared in the New World, the pagans thought horse and rider were one person?" (§7/24) And horses are, Dora tells Dysart, "in the Bible, of course. 'He saith among the trumpets, Ha, ha'" (§7/24). Dora's quotation comes, she tells Dysart, from "the Book of Job [39:25]. Such a noble passage" (§7/24).

3.7 QUEER

1. On queerly embodied differences, see Judith Butler, "Remarks on 'Queer Bonds,'" *GLQ* 17, nos. 2–3 (2011): 381–87; Alison Kafer, *Feminist, Queer, Crip* (Bloomington: Indiana University Press, 2013); and Tavia Nyong'o, *Afro-Fabulations: The Queer Drama of Black Life* (New York: New York University Press, 2019).
2. Queer "values ways," Eve Kosofsky Sedgwick writes, "in which meanings and institutions can be at loose ends with each other, crossing all kinds of boundaries rather than reinforcing them" (*The Weather in Proust* [Durham, NC: Duke University Press, 2011], 200).
3. Queer works as a praxis that, David Halperin writes, "destabilizes the very constitution of identity" (*Saint Foucault: Towards a Gay Hagiography* [Oxford: Oxford University Press, 1995], 96–97).
4. "The 'I' that I am," Judith Butler writes, "finds itself at once constituted by norms and dependent on them but also endeavors to live in ways that maintain a critical and transformative relation to them" (*Undoing Gender* [New York: Routledge, 2004], 3). Queer acts, Vinciane Despret writes, "to transform habits, transform relations to norms, to oneself and others, and to open possibilities" (*What Would Animals Say If We Asked the*

Right Questions?, trans. Brett Buchanan [Minneapolis: University of Minnesota Press, 2016], 137). It makes ways "to open oneself up," Despret writes, "to new *agencements* of desire, to cultivate an appetite for metamorphoses, and to forge multiple affiliations" (*What Would Animals Say If We Asked the Right Questions?*, 137). On queer, cross-species relations, see Natalie Corinne Hansen, "Humans, Horses, and Hormones: (Trans) Gendering Cross-Species Relationships," *WSQ* 36, nos. 3–4 (2008): 87–105.

5. Queer "works," Sue-Ellen Case writes, "not at the site of gender but at the site of ontology, to shift the ground of being" (*Feminist and Queer Performance: Critical Strategies* [New York: Palgrave Macmillan, 2009], 68). Then "queer becomes," Sara Ahmed writes, "a matter of how things appear, how they gather, how they perform, to create the edges of spaces and worlds" (*Queer Phenomenology: Orientations, Objects, Others* [Durham, NC: Duke University Press, 2006], 167).

6. Queer "concerns our ways," Vinciane Despret writes, "of entering into relations with this world and, among these relations, of knowing and practicing this knowledge" (*What Would Animals Say If We Asked the Right Questions?*, 135). These ways of knowing strike us, in Lauren Berlant and Michael Warner's words, "as knowledge central to living" ("What Does Queer Theory Teach Us about *X*?," *PMLA* 110, no. 3 [1995]: 348).

7. "If the term 'queer,'" Judith Butler writes, "is to be a site of collective contestation, the point of departure for a set of critical reflections and future imaginings, it will have to remain that which is, in the present, never fully owned, but always and only redeployed, twisted, queered from a prior usage and in the direction of urgent and expanding political purposes" ("Critically Queer," *GLQ* 1, no. 1 [1993]: 19).

3.8 NUDE

1. Vulnerability names, in Judith Butler's words, "the sense of 'exposure' implied by precarity" ("Rethinking Vulnerability and Resistance," in *Vulnerability in Resistance*, ed. Judith Butler, Zeynep Gambetti, and Leticia Sabsay [Durham, NC: Duke University Press, 2016], 14). "Vulnerability is about," Athena Athanasiou writes, "the abiding and vital potentiality of being affected by others and of owing ourselves to others" (Judith Butler and Athena Athanasiou, *Dispossession: The Performative in the Political* [Malden, MA: Polity, 2013], 158). So "we cannot understand bodily vulnerability," Butler writes, "outside this conception of social and material relations" ("Rethinking Vulnerability and Resistance," 16). "It is difficult," Kent Brintnall writes, "to face our limitations, to admit our vulnerability" (*Ecce Homo: The Male-Body-in-Pain as Redemptive Figure* [Chicago: University of Chicago Press, 2011], 63). "But our unwillingness to do so," Brintnall writes, "prevents us from genuinely encountering the other" (*Ecce Homo*, 63). And "what is at stake in response-ability toward human vulnerability and precarity," Athanasiou writes, is "an 'insurrection at the level of ontology,' that is, the constant questioning of conditions in which the human is determined by normative and normalizing regimes of intelligibility in terms of gender, sexuality, race, nationality, class" (Butler and Athanasiou, *Dispossession*, 119).

2. “In the end,” Georges Bataille writes, “everything puts me at risk, I remain suspended, stripped” (*The Unfinished System of Nonknowledge*, ed. Stuart Kendall, trans. Michelle Kendall and Stuart Kendall [Minneapolis: University of Minnesota Press, 2001], 98). “And the depths of the world opened,” Bataille writes, “what I see and what I know no longer have any meaning, any limits, and I will stop myself only after having advanced the furthest that I can” (*The Unfinished System of Nonknowledge*, 98).
3. “To be a body,” Judith Butler writes, “is to be this very exposure” (“Remarks on ‘Queer Bonds,’” *GLQ* 17, nos. 2–3 [2011]: 382). “To be a body,” Anne Dufourmantelle writes, “is also to be nude” (*In Praise of Risk*, trans. Steven Miller [New York: Fordham University Press, 2019], 75).
4. “Nudity,” Jean-Luc Nancy and Federico Ferrari write, “is not a being. It is not even a quality” (*Being Nude: The Skin of Images*, trans. Anne O’Byrne and Carlie Anglemire [New York: Fordham University Press, 2014], 29). Nudity, Nancy and Ferrari write, “is always a relation, several simultaneous relations” (*Being Nude*, 29). “We can,” Giorgio Agamben writes, “experience nudity only as a denuding and a baring, never as a form or a stable possession” (*Nudities*, trans. David Kishik and Stefan Pedatella [Stanford, CA: Stanford University Press, 2011], 65 [translation modified]).

4.2 PASSION

1. A passion involves, Jacques Derrida writes, “the endurance of an indeterminate or undecidable limit” (*Demeure*, trans. Elizabeth Rottenberg [Stanford, CA: Stanford University Press, 2000], 28). On passion in *Equus*, with attention to pedagogy, see my “Performing Religiously between Passion and Resistance,” *Journal for Cultural and Religious Theory* 12, no. 2 (2012): 69–84.
2. This knotting is, Jean-Luc Nancy writes, “no *thing*, nothing but the putting in relation that supposes at once proximity and distance, attachment and detachment” (*The Sense of the World*, trans. Jeffrey Librett [Minneapolis: University of Minnesota Press, 1997], 111 [translation modified]). “The knot,” Mary-Jane Rubenstein writes, “is no thing at all but rather the sort of twisted ‘not’ that never returns to itself” (*Strange Wonder: The Closure of Metaphysics and the Opening of Awe* [New York: Columbia University Press, 2008], 119). “If one were,” Jacques Derrida writes, “to unravel the lines of force that semantically traverse the word ‘passion,’ one would discover at least *seven* knotted trajectories” (*Demeure*, 25). A Christian trajectory is among them. A passion has, for us and for *Equus*, Christianized histories.
3. “The possibility of unbinding is also,” Jacques Derrida writes, “the only condition of possibility for binding” (*Resistances of Psychoanalysis*, trans. Peggy Kamuf, Pascale-Anne Brault, and Michael Naas [Stanford, CA: Stanford University Press, 1998], 33).
4. Analysis names, Jacques Derrida writes, a “methodological operation of unknotting and technique of untying” (*Resistances of Psychoanalysis*, 15).
5. Passion, Anne Dufourmantelle writes, “is espousing a movement that dispossesses and reveals you at the same time” (*In Praise of Risk*, trans. Steven Miller [New York:

Fordham University Press, 2019], 18). "Passion," Dufourmantelle writes, "is the very substance of risk" (*In Praise of Risk*, 18). It's "our capacity," Dufourmantelle writes, "to imagine, to be astonished, to be disappointed, impressed, or undone by something inside us that compels us to love this skin, this gaze, this accent" (*In Praise of Risk*, 18).

6. A knot of passion, "in being tied," in Jean-Luc Nancy's words, "ceaselessly makes the inside pass outside, each into (or by way of) the other, the outside inside" (*The Sense of the World*, 111). Maybe that's why *différance* might be, Jacques Derrida writes, "another name for 'passion'" (*Demeure*, 27).
7. "An unseen wife and a friendly magistrate," Marla Carlson writes, "wrap Martin Dysart within a superficially heterosexual economy as a screen for his desire flowing toward a 'primitive' exaltation" (*Affect, Animals, and Autists: Feeling around the Edges of the Human in Performance* [Ann Arbor: University of Michigan Press, 2018], 28).

4.3 PAIN

1. The English Touring Theatre's 2019 production stressed this painful scene. It lit the stage in purple hues. Alan's hospital bed had a trampoline in place of a mattress. Nurses (played by the actors who played Nugget and Dalton) wheeled the bed, with Alan in it, onstage. Holding Alan's limbs, the nurses bounced Alan's contorting body—higher and higher. They stopped abruptly when, *Equus* tells us, "*the boy gives a terrible cry*—EK!—*and wakes up*" (§8/29). When they stopped, a white spotlight replaced the purple glow.
2. "The fantasy of eradicating pain, suffering, and death," Kent Brintnall writes, "is understandably seductive" (*Ecce Homo: The Male-Body-in-Pain as Redemptive Figure* [Chicago: University of Chicago Press, 2011], 63). "But it nourishes," Brintnall writes, "problematic conceptions of what it means to be a subject, a human person, an agent in the world" (*Ecce Homo*, 63). On relations of religion, bodies, and pain, see Georges Bataille, *Inner Experience*, trans. Stuart Kendall (Albany: State University of New York Press, 2014), 37–66; and Émile Durkheim, *The Elementary Forms of Religious Life*, trans. Karen E. Fields (New York: Free Press, 1995), 316–21.
3. See Karl Marx, "Toward a Critique of Hegel's *Philosophy of Right*: Introduction," trans. Loyd D. Easton and Kurt H. Guddat, in *Selected Writings*, ed. Lawrence H. Simon (Indianapolis: Hackett, 1994), 28. Reading Marx's text contextually would take account of economies, colonialisms, and racisms involved in nineteenth-century opium trades. (Marx's choice of drug is specific. In Intro, we discuss this specificity: *Why, specifically, opium?*)
4. Religious ideas, Sigmund Freud writes, "are illusions, fulfilling the oldest, most powerful, most pressing desires of the human race" (*The Future of an Illusion*, trans. J. A. Underwood [London: Penguin, 2008], §6, 36). And "the criticism of religion," Karl Marx writes, "disillusions man so that he thinks, acts, and shapes his reality like a disillusioned man who has come to his senses" ("Toward a Critique of Hegel's *Philosophy of Right*," 28).
5. "The most interesting methods of preventing suffering," Sigmund Freud writes, "are

those that seek to influence one's own constitution" (*Civilization and Its Discontents*, trans. David McLintock [London: Penguin, 2002], §2, 16). And "the crudest, but also the most effective, method of influencing our constitution," Freud writes, "is the chemical one—intoxication" (*Civilization and Its Discontents*, §2, 16).

6. Dysart, Madeleine MacMurraugh-Kavanagh writes, "understands that this amputation [of Equus from Alan] is both destructive and should not be demanded" (*Peter Shaffer: Theatre and Drama* [London: Macmillan, 1998], 114). Dysart's difficulty, MacMurraugh-Kavanagh writes, "is that he can see in Hesther's philosophy and in Alan's psyche 'two kinds of Right'" (*Peter Shaffer*, 115).
7. *Equus*'s end isn't the first time Hesther tells Dysart these things. (That makes this later time a reprisal, or reenactment, of an earlier scene.) Earlier in *Equus*, Hesther tells Dysart that Alan has "been in pain for most of his life" (§25/80). "And you," Hesther tells Dysart, "can take it away" (§25/80). "That simply has to be," Hesther tells Dysart, "enough for you" (§25/80). That, Madeleine MacMurraugh-Kavanagh writes, "is 'enough' for Hesther" (*Peter Shaffer*, 114). Dysart, MacMurraugh-Kavanagh writes, "questions his role as social agent; Hesther questions only her fitness to fulfill it, not the role itself" (*Peter Shaffer*, 115).
8. "Dysart has made his own pain," Neil Timm writes, "by helping to alleviate Alan's" ("*Equus* as a Modern Tragedy," *Philological Papers* 25 [1979]: 133).

4.4 NORMAL

1. This ritual treats "sexuality," in Michel Foucault's words, "as the correlation of a domain of knowledge, a type of normativity, and a mode of relation to the self" ("Preface to *The History of Sexuality*, Volume Two," trans. William Smock, in *Ethics: Subjectivity and Truth*, ed. Paul Rabinow [New York: New Press, 1997], 200). Sexuality, Foucault writes, "kept as its nucleus the singular ritual of obligatory and exhaustive confession, which in the Christian West was the first technique for producing the truth of sex" (*History of Sexuality*, vol. 1, trans. Robert Hurley [New York: Vintage, 1990], 68). Confession "and its effects," Foucault writes, "were recoded as therapeutic operations" (*History of Sexuality*, vol. 1, 67 [translation modified]). On Foucault and *Equus*, see Theodore D. George, "The Disruption of Health: Shaffer, Foucault, and 'the Normal,'" *Journal of Medical Humanities* 20, no. 4 (1999): 231–45.
2. At least Dysart tries to do these things. But he's unsure of success. "When Equus leaves—*if he leaves at all*," Dysart tells Alan, "it will be with your intestines in his teeth" (§35/108 [my emphasis]). If Equus leaves, he'll do so inverting Dysart's Normal-ritual. A divinity, not a priest, will excise parts of Alan. And they'll be divinely valued, not devalued, parts.

4.5 TRAGEDY

1. "All tragedy," Eric Hayot writes, "is a meditation on tragedy" (*On Literary Worlds* [Oxford: Oxford University Press, 2012], 71).
2. "Do you want," Anne Carson writes, "to go down to the pits of yourself alone? Not much" (*Grief Lessons: Four Plays by Euripides*, trans. Anne Carson [New York: New York Review Books, 2008], 7). So you watch actors, Carson writes, "act out the present or possible organization of your nature" (*Grief Lessons*, 7). Doing so, "you can," Carson writes, "be aware of your own awareness of this nature as you never are at the moment of experience" (*Grief Lessons*, 7). "Tragedy leads to self-questioning," Simon Goldhill writes, "through the pain of others" (*Love, Sex, and Tragedy: How the Ancient World Shapes Our Lives* [Chicago: University of Chicago Press, 2004], 229).
3. There are many other responses. Aristotle's is an influential one. "Tragedy," Aristotle writes, "is an imitation of an action serious and complete, having magnitude, in language made pleasing in distinct forms in its separate parts, imitating people acting and not using narration, accomplishing by means of pity and fear the cleansing of these states of feeling" (*Poetics*, trans. Joe Sachs [Newburyport, MA: Focus, 2006], 1449b24–28). But its influence is a problem. "Aristotle's way of reading tragedy," Ruth Scodel writes, "is profoundly Aristotelian" (*An Introduction to Greek Tragedy* [Cambridge: Cambridge University Press, 2010], 7). And "most of us," Scodel writes, "are not actually followers of Aristotle" (*An Introduction to Greek Tragedy*, 7). I'm not, since Aristotle's sense of tragedy would exclude *Equus*, or any metatheatrical play. For some others' responses, see Georges Bataille, *The Unfinished System of Nonknowledge*, ed. Stuart Kendall, trans. Michelle Kendall and Stuart Kendall (Minneapolis: University of Minnesota Press, 2001), 119–28; Adrian Poole, *Tragedy: A Very Short Introduction* (Oxford: Oxford University Press, 2005); and Peter Szondi, *An Essay on the Tragic*, trans. Paul Fleming (Stanford, CA: Stanford University Press, 2002).
4. "Why does tragedy exist?" Anne Carson writes. "Because you are full of rage. Why are you full of rage? Because you are full of grief" (*Grief Lessons*, 7). "Grief and rage—you need to contain that," Carson writes, "to put a frame around it, where it can play itself out without you or your kin having to die" (*Grief Lessons*, 7).
5. "The entire tragic tradition, from [ancient] Greek tragedy onward," Ruth Scodel writes, "concerns itself with some core issues: the vulnerability of human life; the value of facing the limits of our control with courage; and the powerful, sometimes inescapable, effects of our decisions" (*An Introduction to Greek Tragedy*, 7).
6. "The play of the theatre," Howard Barker writes, "asks[:] how shall we live?" (*Death, the One and the Art of Theatre* [New York: Routledge, 2005], 94). "Tragedy answers the question," Barker writes, "in the very act of exposing the way into death. It draws death back into life, and consequently alters life" (*Death, the One and the Art of Theatre*, 94).
7. "Tragedy," Howard Barker writes, "is not a demonstration" (*Death, the One and the Art of Theatre*, 45). Tragedy, Barker writes, "is a terrible ignorance that admits itself" (*Death, the One and the Art of Theatre*, 45).
8. For a range of responses, see Dennis A. Klein, *Peter Shaffer*, rev. ed. (New York: Twayne,

1993), 118; Gene A. Plunka, *Peter Shaffer: Roles, Rites, and Rituals in the Theatre* (Rutherford, NJ: Fairleigh Dickinson University Press, 1988), 166–67; and Neil Timm, "*Equus* as a Modern Tragedy," *Philological Papers* 25 (1979): 133–34.

4.6 SACRIFICE

1. "To sacrifice," Georges Bataille writes, "is not to kill but to relinquish and to give" (*Theory of Religion*, trans. Robert Hurley [New York: Zone Books, 1989], 48–49). Sacrifice is "a religious act," Henri Hubert and Marcel Mauss write, "which, through the consecration of the victim, modifies the condition of the moral person who accomplishes it or that of certain objects with which he [or she or they] is concerned" (*Sacrifice: Its Nature and Function*, trans. W. D. Halls [Chicago: University of Chicago Press, 1981], 13).
2. Analyzing these actions and transactions is one thing. Inventing them is another. Doing the latter is difficult. It shows us how complex sacrifice can be. To study these complexities in Intro, we collectively invent a sacrifice. A student volunteers to be sacrificed. (Don't worry. We don't *really* sacrifice a student. In Intro, inventing a sacrifice is a learning, not a ritual, activity.) Everyone else spends up to twenty minutes working out this sacrifice's details. Who sacrifices? To whom? For what? How, specifically (site, time, instrument, method)? Why? How might we know whether the sacrifice was effective? These questions raise others, about desires and values and relations and limits in our invented context. They're pressing questions for ritualization. Ritualization names, Catherine Bell writes, "a strategic *way* of acting" (*Ritual Theory, Ritual Practice* [Oxford: Oxford University Press, 2009], 7). It's a "way of acting," Bell writes, "that sets itself off from other ways of acting by virtue of the way in which it does what it does" (*Ritual Theory, Ritual Practice*, 140). Ritualization involves, Bell writes, "the formal 'modeling' of valued relationships so as to promote legitimation and internalization of those relations and their values" (*Ritual Theory, Ritual Practice*, 89). In Intro, our inventing-a-sacrifice activity enacts an experiment in ritualization.
3. This partial death might be, in Neil Timm's words, "the living death of the Normal" ("*Equus* as a Modern Tragedy," *Philological Papers* 25 [1979]: 129).
4. When this sacrifice culminates, Alan is nude. That's performatively crucial. "The image of a human sacrifice," Peter Shaffer writes, "which was intended although only lightly stressed, vanished entirely with the assumption of a sweater and jeans" (*The Collected Plays of Peter Shaffer* [New York: Harmony Books, 1982], xv).
5. Normalizing domesticates. And "sacrifice is," Jonathan Z. Smith writes, "an exaggeration of domestication" (*Relating Religion: Essays in the Study of Religion* [Chicago: University of Chicago Press, 2004], 152).
6. Dysart doesn't limit his "thousand local Gods" to animate animals or divinities. He counts among them, he tells Hesther, "spirits of certain trees, certain curves of brick walls, certain chip shops, if you like, and slate roofs" (§18/59). On pantheistic possibilities, see Mary-Jane Rubenstein, *Pantheologies: Gods, Worlds, Monsters* (New York: Columbia University Press, 2018).

7. "At the moment of the sacrifice," Alphonso Lingis writes, "participants find their identity slashed with the knife" (*Violence and Splendor* [Evanston, IL: Northwestern University Press, 2011], 88). So a sacrifice might be akin to an ethic. Each might enact, in Jill Robbins's words, "a radical putting into question of the self and the subject in the presence of the other" ("Sacrifice," in *Critical Terms for Religious Studies*, ed. Mark C. Taylor [Chicago: University of Chicago Press, 1998], 291).

4.7 ENDING

1. *Equus*, John Clair Watson writes, "does not end with a solution, only with questions" ("The Ritual Plays of Peter Shaffer" [PhD diss., University of Oregon, 1987], 148). "The audience is allowed," Watson writes, "the temporary solace of recognizing their shared limitation, but each member is left to deal with his or her [or their] own sharp chain" ("The Ritual Plays of Peter Shaffer," 148). This sharp chain might be "the bridle," Patrick Hutchings writes, "that being in the world puts in all our mouths" ("*Equus* and the Concept of Worship," *Sophia* 33, no. 1 [1994]: 30).

4.8 VALUE

1. Critique, Judith Butler writes, "does not return us to already established frameworks and norms" ("The Sensibility of Critique," in *Is Critique Secular? Blasphemy, Injury, and Free Speech*, ed. Talal Asad, Wendy Brown, Judith Butler, and Saba Mahmood, rev. ed. [New York: Fordham University Press, 2013], 108). It calls "into question," Butler writes, "established frameworks of evaluation" ("The Sensibility of Critique," 108). Critique names, Butler writes, "an ungrounded inquiry into the legitimacy of existing grounds" ("Critique, Dissent, Disciplinarity," *Critical Inquiry* 35, no. 4 [2009]: 786). ("Ungrounded" means, Butler writes, "that what form it takes is not knowable or predictable on the basis of established norms" ["Critique, Dissent, Disciplinarity," 786]). Critique involves, Butler writes, "questioning the limits imposed upon the askable" ("Critique, Dissent, Disciplinarity," 787).
2. Critique can mark, Heather Love writes, "a commitment to tracing social arrangements in-the-making" ("The Temptations: Donna Haraway, Feminist Objectivity, and the Problem of Critique," in *Critique and Postcritique*, ed. Elizabeth S. Anker and Rita Felski [Durham, NC: Duke University Press, 2017], 69). And "the careful examination of the world as it appears," Love writes, "does not imply a capitulation to *the way things are*" ("The Temptations," 69).
3. Critique isn't, in Saba Mahmood's words, "about successfully demolishing your opponent's position and exposing the implausibility of her [or his or their] argument" (*Politics of Piety: The Islamic Revival and the Feminist Subject*, rev. ed. [Princeton, NJ: Princeton University Press, 2012], 36). That, Mahmood writes, "is a very limited and

weak understanding of the notion of critique" (*Politics of Piety*, 36). I think it's a misunderstanding. The acts Mahmood describes are acts of criticism, not critique. Critique acts differently. It "leaves open," Mahmood writes, "the possibility that we might also be remade in the process of engaging another's worldview, that we might come to learn things that we did not already know before we undertook the engagement" (*Politics of Piety*, 36–37). Mahmood might (also) be describing what we call performance, or what we call pedagogy (or what I call writing).

4. "People have taken," Friedrich Nietzsche writes, "the *value* of these 'values' as given, as factual, as beyond all questioning" (*On the Genealogy of Morality*, ed. Keith Ansell-Pearson, trans. Carol Diethe, 3rd ed. [Cambridge: Cambridge University Press, 2017], 8). "So let us give voice to this new demand," Nietzsche writes: "*the value of these values should itself, for once, be examined*" (*On the Genealogy of Morality*, 8).

ENCORE

1. Patti Smith, *Horses*, Arista 07822-18827-2, 1996, compact disc (originally released in 1975). For the lyrics of "Land," see Patti Smith, *Patti Smith Complete: 1975–2006; Lyrics, Reflections, and Notes for the Future* (New York: Harper Perennial, 2006), 51–58. All quotations in this Encore cite these lyrics. On "Land," see Philip Shaw, *Horses* (New York: Continuum, 2008), 123–35.

REFERENCES

Abel, Lionel. *Tragedy and Metatheatre: Essays on Dramatic Form.* New York: Holmes and Meier, 2003.

Agamben, Giorgio. *Nudities.* Translated by David Kishik and Stefan Pedatella. Stanford, CA: Stanford University Press, 2011.

Ahmed, Sara. *Queer Phenomenology: Orientations, Objects, Others.* Durham, NC: Duke University Press, 2006.

Akstens, Thomas. "Redression as a Structural Imperative in Shaffer's *Equus*." *Journal of Dramatic Theory and Criticism* 6, no. 2 (1992): 89–98.

Althusser, Louis. *Lenin and Philosophy, and Other Essays.* Translated by Ben Brewster. New York: Monthly Review Press, 2001.

Anker, Elizabeth S., and Rita Felski, eds. *Critique and Postcritique.* Durham, NC: Duke University Press, 2017.

Aristotle. *Nicomachean Ethics.* Translated by Joe Sachs. Newburyport, MA: Focus, 2002.

———. *Poetics.* Translated by Joe Sachs. Newburyport, MA: Focus, 2006.

Artaud, Antonin. *The Theatre and Its Double.* Translated by Mary Caroline Richards. New York: Grove, 1958.

Attridge, Derek. *The Singularity of Literature.* New York: Routledge, 2004.

Auslander, Philip, ed. *Performance: Critical Concepts in Literary and Cultural Studies.* New York: Routledge, 2003.

Baldwin, Helene L. "*Equus*: Theatre of Cruelty or Theatre of Sensationalism?" *West Virginia University Philosophical Papers* 25 (1979): 118–27.

Ball, David. *Backwards and Forwards: A Technical Manual for Reading Plays.* Carbondale: Southern Illinois University Press, 1983.

Barad, Karen. *Meeting the Universe Halfway: Quantum Physics and the Entanglement of Matter and Meaning.* Durham, NC: Duke University Press, 2007.

Barker, Howard. *Death, the One and the Art of Theatre.* New York: Routledge, 2005.

Barnes, Clive. "*Equus* a New Success on Broadway." *New York Times,* 25 October 1974.

Bataille, Georges. *Inner Experience.* Translated by Stuart Kendall. Albany: State University of New York Press, 2014.

———. *Theory of Religion.* Translated by Robert Hurley. New York: Zone Books, 1989.

———. *The Unfinished System of Nonknowledge.* Edited by Stuart Kendall. Translated by

Michelle Kendall and Stuart Kendall. Minneapolis: University of Minnesota Press, 2001.

Bell, Catherine. "Performance." In Taylor, *Critical Terms for Religious Studies*, 205–24.

———. *Ritual Theory, Ritual Practice*. Oxford: Oxford University Press, 2009.

Bennett, Andrew, and Nicholas Royle. *This Thing Called Literature: Reading, Thinking, Writing*. New York: Routledge, 2015.

Benoist, Jocelyn. "Judgment and Beyond." *Critical Inquiry* 45, no. 2 (2019): 260–79.

Berger, John. *Ways of Seeing*. New York: Penguin, 1977.

Berlant, Lauren. "On the Case." *Critical Inquiry* 33, no. 4 (2007): 663–72.

———. "What Does It Matter Who One Is?" *Critical Inquiry* 34, no. 1 (2007): 1–4.

Berlant, Lauren, and Michael Warner. "What Does Queer Theory Teach Us about *X*?" *PMLA* 110, no. 3 (1995): 343–49.

Billington, Michael. "Peter Shaffer's Homoerotic Classic Is Exhilarating." *Guardian* (US edition), 24 February 2019.

Boal, Augusto. *Aesthetics of the Oppressed*. Translated by Adrian Jackson. New York: Routledge, 2006.

Boas, Frederick S. *Shakespeare and His Predecessors*. London: John Murray, 1910.

Boscaljon, Daniel, and Alan Levinovitz, eds. *Teaching Religion and Literature*. New York: Routledge, 2019.

Bouchard, Larry D. *Tragic Method and Tragic Theology: Evil in Contemporary Drama and Religious Thought*. University Park: Pennsylvania State University Press, 1989.

Bowden, Hugh. *Mystery Cults of the Ancient World*. Princeton, NJ: Princeton University Press, 2010.

Brantley, Ben. "In the Darkness of the Stable." *New York Times*, 25 September 2008.

Braun, Willi, and Russell T. McCutcheon, eds. *Guide to the Study of Religion*. London: Cassell, 2000.

Brecht, Bertold. *Brecht on Theatre: The Development of an Aesthetic*. Edited and translated by John Willett. New York: Hill and Wang, 1964.

Brintnall, Kent L. *Ecce Homo: The Male-Body-in-Pain as Redemptive Figure*. Chicago: University of Chicago Press, 2011.

Burkert, Walter. *Ancient Mystery Cults*. Cambridge, MA: Harvard University Press, 1989.

Butler, Judith. "Critically Queer." *GLQ* 1, no. 1 (1993): 17–32.

———. "Critique, Dissent, Disciplinarity." *Critical Inquiry* 35, no. 4 (2009): 773–95.

———. "Disruptive Kinship." In the discussion "Affinities: Villa Gillet's Walls and Bridges Series," with Hélène Cixous and Avital Ronell, New School, 24 October 2011. Video, 1:49:18. http://youtu.be/8k91WwJIhl8.

———. *Giving an Account of Oneself*. New York: Fordham University Press, 2005.

———. "Performative Acts and Gender Constitution: An Essay in Phenomenology and Feminist Theory." *Theatre Journal* 40, no. 4 (1988): 519–31.

———. "Remarks on 'Queer Bonds.'" *GLQ* 17, nos. 2–3 (2011): 381–87.

———. "Rethinking Vulnerability and Resistance." In *Vulnerability in Resistance*, edited by Judith Butler, Zeynep Gambetti, and Leticia Sabsay, 12–27. Durham, NC: Duke University Press, 2016.

———. "The Sensibility of Critique." In *Is Critique Secular? Blasphemy, Injury, and Free*

Speech, edited by Talal Asad, Wendy Brown, Judith Butler, and Saba Mahmood, 95–130. Rev. ed. New York: Fordham University Press, 2013.
———. *Undoing Gender*. New York: Routledge, 2004.
Butler, Judith, and Athena Athanasiou. *Dispossession: The Performative in the Political*. Malden, MA: Polity, 2013.
Carlson, Marla. *Affect, Animals, and Autists: Feeling around the Edges of the Human in Performance*. Ann Arbor: University of Michigan Press, 2018.
Carlson, Marvin. *Performance: A Critical Introduction*. 3rd ed. New York: Routledge, 2018.
Case, Sue-Ellen. *Feminist and Queer Performance: Critical Strategies*. New York: Palgrave Macmillan, 2009.
Certeau, Michel de. *The Practice of Everyday Life*. Translated by Steven Rendall. Berkeley: University of California Press, 1984.
———. "What We Do When We Believe." Translated by Richard Miller. In *On Signs*, edited by Marshall Blonsky, 192–202. Baltimore: Johns Hopkins University Press, 1985.
Chaudhuri, Una. "The Spectator in Drama/Drama in the Spectator." *Modern Drama* 27, no. 3 (1984): 281–98.
———. *The Stage Lives of Animals: Zooësis and Performance*. New York: Routledge, 2016.
Chidester, David. *Religion: Material Dynamics*. Oakland: University of California Press, 2018.
Chuh, Kandice. *The Difference Aesthetics Makes: The Humanities "after Man."* Durham, NC: Duke University Press, 2019.
Conquergood, Dwight. "Performance Studies: Interventions and Radical Research." *TDR* 46, no. 2 (2002): 145–56.
Conroy, Colette. *Theatre and the Body*. New York: Palgrave Macmillan, 2010.
Crawley, Ashon T. *The Lonely Letters*. Durham, NC: Duke University Press, 2020.
Deleuze, Gilles. *The Logic of Sense*. Translated by Constantin V. Boundas. New York: Columbia University Press, 1990.
Derrida, Jacques. *Aporias*. Translated by Thomas Dutoit. Stanford, CA: Stanford University Press, 1993.
———. "A Certain Impossible Possibility of Saying the Event." Translated by Gila Walker. *Critical Inquiry* 33, no. 2 (2007): 441–61.
———. *Demeure*. Translated by Elizabeth Rottenberg. Stanford, CA: Stanford University Press, 2000.
———. "Faith and Knowledge: The Two Sources of 'Religion' at the Limits of Reason Alone." Translated by Samuel Weber. In *Religion*, edited by Jacques Derrida and Gianni Vattimo, 1–78. Stanford, CA: Stanford University Press, 1998.
———. *Of Grammatology*. Translated by Gayatri Chakravorty Spivak. Rev. ed. Baltimore: Johns Hopkins University Press, 1997.
———. *Resistances of Psychoanalysis*. Translated by Peggy Kamuf, Pascale-Anne Brault, and Michael Naas. Stanford, CA: Stanford University Press, 1998.
———. *The Truth in Painting*. Translated by Geoff Bennington and Ian McLeod. Chicago: University of Chicago Press, 1987.

———. *Without Alibi*. Edited and translated by Peggy Kamuf. Stanford, CA: Stanford University Press, 2002.

———. *Writing and Difference*. Translated by Alan Bass. Chicago: University of Chicago Press, 1978.

Derrida, Jacques, and Derek Attridge. "'This Strange Institution Called Literature.'" Translated by Geoffrey Bennington and Rachel Bowlby. In *Acts of Literature*, edited by Derek Attridge, 33–75. New York: Routledge, 1992.

Despret, Vinciane. "The Body We Care For: Figures of Anthropo-zoo-genesis." *Body and Society* 10, nos. 2–3 (2004): 111–34.

———. *What Would Animals Say If We Asked the Right Questions?* Translated by Brett Buchanan. Minneapolis: University of Minnesota Press, 2016.

Dickinson, Colby. *Words Fail: Theology, Poetry, and the Challenge of Representation*. New York: Fordham University Press, 2017.

Dufourmantelle, Anne. *In Praise of Risk*. Translated by Steven Miller. New York: Fordham University Press, 2019.

Durkheim, Émile. *The Elementary Forms of Religious Life*. Translated by Karen E. Fields. New York: Free Press, 1995.

Ebner, I. Dean. "The Double Crisis of Sexuality and Worship in Shaffer's *Equus*." *Christianity and Literature* 31, no. 2 (1982): 29–47.

Euripides. *Grief Lessons: Four Plays by Euripides*. Translated by Anne Carson. New York: New York Review Books, 2008.

Fanon, Frantz. *Black Skin, White Masks*. Translated by Richard Philcox. New York: Grove, 2008.

Felman, Shoshana. *The Scandal of the Speaking Body: Don Juan with J. L. Austin, or Seduction in Two Languages*. Translated by Catherine Porter. Stanford, CA: Stanford University Press, 2002.

Fink, Eugen. *Play as Symbol of the World*. Translated by Ian Alexander Moore and Christopher Turner. Bloomington: Indiana University Press, 2016.

Fischer-Lichte, Erika. "The Concept of Performance." In *The Routledge Introduction to Theatre and Performance Studies*, edited by Minou Arjomand and Ramona Masse, translated by Minou Arjomand, 18–46. New York: Routledge, 2014.

———. "Performance as Event—Reception as Transformation." In *Theorising Performance: Greek Drama, Cultural History and Critical Practice*, edited by Edith Hall and Stephen Harrop, 29–42. New York: Bloomsbury, 2013.

———. *Theatre, Sacrifice, Ritual: Exploring Forms of Political Theatre*. New York: Routledge, 2005.

———. *The Transformative Power of Performance: A New Aesthetics*. Translated by Saskya Iris Jain. New York: Routledge, 2008.

Foucault, Michel. *History of Sexuality*. Vol. 1. Translated by Robert Hurley. New York: Vintage, 1990.

———. "Preface to *The History of Sexuality*, Volume 2." Translated by William Smock. In *Ethics: Subjectivity and Truth*, edited by Paul Rabinow, 199–205. New York: New Press, 1997.

———. "A Preface to Transgression." Translated by Donald F. Bouchard and Sherry

Simon. In *Aesthetics, Epistemology and Method*, edited by James D. Faubion, 69–87. New York: New Press, 1998.

Freeman, Barbara. *Staging the Gaze: Postmodernism, Psychoanalysis, and Shakespearean Comedy*. Ithaca, NY: Cornell University Press, 1991.

Freeman, Elizabeth. "Queer Belongings." In *A Companion to Lesbian, Gay, Bisexual, Transgender, and Queer Studies*, edited by George C. Haggerty and Molly McGarry, 295–314. Malden, MA: Blackwell, 2007.

Freud, Sigmund. *Civilization and Its Discontents*. Translated by David McLintock. London: Penguin, 2002.

———. *The Future of an Illusion*. Translated by J. A. Underwood. London: Penguin, 2008.

Gasché, Rodolphe. *Of Minimal Things: Studies in the Notion of Relation*. Stanford, CA: Stanford University Press, 1999.

George, Theodore D. "The Disruption of Health: Shaffer, Foucault, and 'the Normal.'" *Journal of Medical Humanities* 20, no. 4 (1999): 231–45.

Gianakaris, C. J. *Peter Shaffer*. London: Macmillan, 1992.

Gill, Sam D. *Dancing Culture Religion*. Lanham, MD: Lexington Books, 2012.

———. "Play." In Braun and McCutcheon, *Guide to the Study of Religion*, 451–62.

———. "Play as Pedagogy." Unpublished manuscript. http://sam-gill.com/PDF/Play%20and%20Pedagogy.pdf.

———. *Storytracking: Texts, Stories, and Histories in Central Australia*. Oxford: Oxford University Press, 1998.

Glissant, Édouard. *Poetics of Relation*. Translated by Betsy Wing. Ann Arbor: University of Michigan Press, 1997.

Goldhill, Simon. *Love, Sex, and Tragedy: How the Ancient World Shapes Our Lives*. Chicago: University of Chicago Press, 2004.

Goldman, Michael. *The Actor's Freedom: Toward a Theory of Drama*. New York: Viking, 1975.

———. *On Drama: Boundaries of Genre, Borders of Self*. Ann Arbor: University of Michigan Press, 2000.

Graver, David. "The Actor's Bodies." *Text and Performance Quarterly* 17, no. 3 (1997): 221–35.

Guest, Kristen, and Monica Mattfeld, eds. *Equestrian Cultures: Horses, Human Society, and the Discourse of Modernity*. Chicago: University of Chicago Press, 2019.

Gussow, Mel. "Shaffer Details a Mind's Journey into *Equus*." *New York Times*, 24 October 1974.

Halperin, David. *Saint Foucault: Towards a Gay Hagiography*. Oxford: Oxford University Press, 1995.

Hammerschlag, Sarah. *Broken Tablets: Levinas, Derrida, and the Literary Afterlife of Religion*. New York: Columbia University Press, 2016.

Hansen, Natalie Corinne. "Horse Stories: Rethinking the Human-Animal Divide." PhD diss., University of California, Santa Cruz, 2009.

———. "Humans, Horses, and Hormones: (Trans) Gendering Cross-Species Relationships." *WSQ* 36, nos. 3–4 (2008): 87–105.

Haraway, Donna J. *Staying with the Trouble: Making Kin in the Chthulucene*. Durham, NC: Duke University Press, 2016.

Harding, Sandra, ed. *The Feminist Standpoint Theory Reader: Intellectual and Political Controversies*. New York: Routledge, 2004.

Hayman, Ronald. *How to Read a Play*. London: Eyre Methuen, 1977.

Hayot, Eric. *On Literary Worlds*. Oxford: Oxford University Press, 2012.

Henricks, Thomas. *Play and the Human Condition*. Urbana: University of Illinois Press, 2015.

Hilton, Julian. *Performance*. London: Macmillan, 1987.

Hogan, Katherine A. "Talking to the Audience: Narrative Characters in Twentieth-Century Drama." PhD diss., St. John's University, 2005.

Hollywood, Amy. *Acute Melancholia, and Other Essays: Mysticism, History, and the Study of Religion*. New York: Columbia University Press, 2016.

hooks, bell. "Performance Practice as a Site of Opposition." In *Let's Get It On: The Politics of Black Performance*, edited by Catherine Ugwa, 210–21. Seattle: Bay View Press, 1995.

Hubert, Henri, and Marcel Mauss. *Sacrifice: Its Nature and Function*. Translated by W. D. Halls. Chicago: University of Chicago Press, 1981.

Hughes, Aaron W. *Comparison: A Critical Primer*. Sheffield, UK: Equinox, 2017.

Hutchings, Patrick. "*Equus* and the Concept of Worship." *Sophia* 33, no. 1 (1994): 14–31.

Jackson, Shannon. "Professing Performance: Disciplinary Genealogies." *TDR* 45, no. 1 (2001): 84–95.

Jen, Huai-Min. "A Lighting Design for *Equus*." MFA thesis, Texas Tech University, 1995.

Johnson, Barbara. *The Feminist Difference: Literature, Psychoanalysis, Race, and Gender*. Cambridge, MA: Harvard University Press, 1998.

Jones, Amelia. *Body Art/Performing the Subject*. Minneapolis: University of Minnesota Press, 1998.

———. "Whiteness." In *Reading Contemporary Performance: Theatricality across Genres*, edited by Meiling Cheng and Gabrielle H. Cody, 278–79. New York: Routledge, 2016.

Kafer, Alison. *Feminist, Queer, Crip*. Bloomington: Indiana University Press, 2013.

Kage, Melanie. "Of Men and Centaurs: Identity and the Relationship of Humans and Horses in Peter Shaffer's *Equus*." MA thesis, Linköping University, 2010.

Kant, Immanuel. *Groundwork of the Metaphysics of Morals*. Edited and translated by Mary Gregor and Jens Timmermann. Rev. ed. Cambridge: Cambridge University Press, 2012.

Kaplan, Morris Bernard. "*Equus*—a Psychiatrist Questions His Priestly Powers." *Hastings Center Report* 5, no. 1 (1975): 9–10.

Kemp, Amanda Denise. "This Black Body in Question." In Phelan and Lane, *The Ends of Performance*, 116–29.

Kirshenblatt-Gimblett, Barbara. "Performance Studies." In *The Performance Studies Reader*, edited by Henry Bial and Sara Brady, 25–36. 3rd ed. New York: Routledge, 2016.

Klein, Dennis A. *Peter Shaffer*. Rev. ed. New York: Twayne, 1993.

Kondo, Dorinne. *Worldmaking: Race, Performance, and the Work of Creativity*. Durham, NC: Duke University Press, 2018.

Kronick, Joseph G. *Derrida and the Future of Literature*. Albany: State University of New York Press, 1999.

Laing, R. D. *The Divided Self*. London: Penguin 2010.

Larson, Catherine. "What Do We Mean When We Talk about Performance? A Metacritical Overview of an Evolving Concept." *Latin American Theatre Review* 45, no. 1 (2011): 23–44.

Lehmann, Hans-Thies. *Postdramatic Theatre*. Translated by Karen Jürs-Munby. New York: Routledge, 2006.

Levinas, Emmanuel. *Otherwise Than Being, or Beyond Essence*. Translated by Alphonso Lingis. Pittsburgh: Duquesne University Press, 1998.

Lewis, George E. "Listening for Freedom with Arnold Davidson." *Critical Inquiry* 45, no. 2 (2019): 434–47.

Lingis, Alphonso. *Violence and Splendor*. Evanston, IL: Northwestern University Press, 2011.

Lofton, Kathryn. *Consuming Religion*. Chicago: University of Chicago Press, 2017.

Lounsberry, Barbara. "'God-Hunting': The Chaos of Worship in Peter Shaffer's *Equus* and *The Royal Hunt of the Sun*." *Modern Drama* 21, no. 1 (1978): 13–28.

Love, Heather. "The Temptations: Donna Haraway, Feminist Objectivity, and the Problem of Critique." In *Critique and Postcritique*, edited by Elizabeth S. Anker and Rita Felski, 50–72. Durham, NC: Duke University Press, 2017.

MacMurraugh-Kavanagh, Madeleine. *Peter Shaffer: Theatre and Drama*. London: Macmillan, 1998.

Madison, D. Soyini, and Judith Hamera. "Performance Studies at the Intersections." In *The Sage Handbook of Performance Studies*, edited by D. Soyini Madison and Judith Hamera, xi–xxv. Thousand Oaks, CA: Sage, 2006.

Mahmood, Saba. *Politics of Piety: The Islamic Revival and the Feminist Subject*. Rev. ed. Princeton, NJ: Princeton University Press, 2012.

Margulis, Lynn, and Dorion Sagan. *What Is Life?* Berkeley: University of California Press, 2000.

Marra, Kim. "Horseback Views: A Queer Hippological Performance." In *Animal Acts: Performing Species Today*, edited by Una Chaudhuri and Holly Hughes, 111–40. Ann Arbor: University of Michigan Press, 2014.

Martin, Luther H. "Comparison." In Braun and McCutcheon, *Guide to the Study of Religion*, 45–56.

Marx, Karl. "Toward a Critique of Hegel's *Philosophy of Right*: Introduction." Translated by Loyd D. Easton and Kurt H. Guddat. In *Selected Writings*, edited by Lawrence Simon, 27–39. Indianapolis: Hackett, 1994.

McHugh, Susan. *Animal Stories: Narrating across Species Lines*. Minneapolis: University of Minnesota Press, 2011.

Merleau-Ponty, Maurice. *The Visible and the Invisible*. Edited by Claude Lefort. Translated by Alphonso Lingis. Evanston, IL: Northwestern University Press, 1968.

Mill, John Stuart. *Utilitarianism*. Edited by George Sher. 2nd ed. Indianapolis: Hackett, 2001.

Miller, David L. *Gods and Games: Toward a Theology of Play*. New York: Harper and Row, 1973.

Miller, J. Hillis. *On Literature*. New York: Routledge, 2002.

Moten, Fred. *In the Break: The Aesthetics of the Black Radical Tradition*. Minneapolis: University of Minnesota Press, 2003.

Muñoz, José Esteban. *Disidentifications: Queers of Color and the Performance of Politics*. Minneapolis: University of Minnesota Press, 1999.

Mustazza, Leonard. "A Jealous God: Ritual and Judgment in Shaffer's *Equus*." *Papers on Language and Literature* 28, no. 2 (1992): 174–84.

Nancy, Jean-Luc. *Being Singular Plural*. Translated by Robert D. Richardson and Anne E. O'Byrne. Stanford, CA: Stanford University Press, 2000.

———. "Body—Theatre." In *Expectation: Philosophy, Literature*, translated by Robert Bononno, 152–64. New York: Fordham University Press, 2018.

———. *The Sense of the World*. Translated by Jeffrey Librett. Minneapolis: University of Minnesota Press, 1997.

Nancy, Jean-Luc, and Federico Ferrari. *Being Nude: The Skin of Images*. Translated by Anne O'Byrne and Carlie Anglemire. New York: Fordham University Press, 2014.

Nelson, Robert S. "Vision." In *Key Terms in Material Religion*, edited by S. Brent Plate, 267–74. New York: Bloomsbury, 2015.

Nietzsche, Friedrich. *The Gay Science*. Edited by Bernard Williams. Translated by Josefine Nauckhoff. Cambridge: Cambridge University Press, 2001.

———. *On the Genealogy of Morality*. Edited by Keith Ansell-Pearson. Translated by Carol Diethe. 3rd ed. Cambridge: Cambridge University Press, 2017.

Noddings, Nel. *Caring: A Relational Approach to Ethics and Moral Education*. 2nd ed. Berkeley: University of California Press, 2013.

Nyong'o, Tavia. *Afro-Fabulations: The Queer Drama of Black Life*. New York: New York University Press, 2019.

Olson, Carl. *Religious Studies: The Key Concepts*. New York: Routledge, 2011.

Orozco, Lourdes. *Theatre and Animals*. London: Red Globe, 2013.

Orozco, Lourdes, and Jennifer Parker-Starbuck, eds. *Performing Animality: Animals in Performance Practices*. New York: Palgrave Macmillan, 2015.

Pao, Angela C. *No Safe Spaces: Re-casting Race, Ethnicity, and Nationality in American Theatre*. Ann Arbor: University of Michigan Press, 2010.

Patton, Kimberley C., and Benjamin C. Ray, eds. *A Magic Still Dwells: Comparative Religion in the Postmodern Age*. Berkeley: University of California Press, 2000.

Phelan, Peggy, and Jill Lane, eds. *The Ends of Performance*. New York: New York University Press, 1998.

Plate, S. Brent, ed. *Key Terms in Material Religion*. New York: Bloomsbury, 2015.

Plunka, Gene A. *Peter Shaffer: Roles, Rites, and Rituals in the Theatre*. Rutherford, NJ: Farleigh Dickinson University Press, 1988.

Poole, Adrian. *Tragedy: A Very Short Introduction*. Oxford: Oxford University Press, 2005.

Poppiti, Kimberly. "Pure Air and Fire: Horses and Dramatic Representations of the Horse on the American Theatrical Stage." PhD diss., New York University, 2003.

Rancière, Jacques. *Aesthetics and Its Discontents*. Translated by Steven Corcoran. Malden, MA: Polity, 2009.

Robbins, Jill. "Sacrifice." In Taylor, *Critical Terms for Religious Studies*, 285–97.

Robert, William. "Pedagogical Cliff-Jumping." *Teaching Theology and Religion* 24, no. 1 (March 2021): 55–64.

———. "Performing Religiously between Passion and Resistance." *Journal for Cultural and Religious Theory* 12, no. 2 (2012): 69–84.

Roberts, Tyler. *Encountering Religion: Responsibility and Criticism after Secularism*. New York: Columbia University Press, 2013.

Rubenstein, Mary-Jane. *Pantheologies: Gods, Worlds, Monsters*. New York: Columbia University Press, 2018.

———. *Strange Wonder: The Closure of Metaphysics and the Opening of Awe*. New York: Columbia University Press, 2008.

———. *Worlds without End: The Many Lives of the Multiverse*. New York: Columbia University Press, 2014.

Sallis, John. *Force of Imagination: The Sense of the Elemental*. Bloomington: Indiana University Press, 2000.

Sandahl, Carrie, and Philip Auslander, eds. *Bodies in Commotion: Disability and Performance*. Ann Arbor: University of Michigan Press, 2005.

Schechner, Richard. *The Future of Ritual: Writings on Culture and Performance*. New York: Routledge, 1993.

———. "What Is Performance Studies Anyway?" In Phelan and Lane, *The Ends of Performance*, 357–62

Scodel, Ruth. *An Introduction to Greek Tragedy*. Cambridge: Cambridge University Press, 2010.

Sedgwick, Eve Kosofsky. *The Weather in Proust*. Durham, NC: Duke University Press, 2011.

Segal, Robert A., and Kocku von Stuckrad, eds. *Vocabulary for the Study of Religion*. Leiden: Brill, 2015.

Shaffer, Peter. "The Cannibal Theatre." *Atlantic Monthly* 206 (October 1960): 48–50.

———. *The Collected Plays of Peter Shaffer*. New York: Harmony Books, 1982.

———. *Equus*. London: Andre Deutsch, 1973.

———. *Equus*. Edited by T. S. Pearce. Essex, UK: Longman, 1983.

———. *Equus*. New York: Scribner, 2005.

———. "A Personal Essay." In *Equus*, edited by T. S. Pearce, vi–x. Essex, UK: Longman, 1983.

Shaw, Philip. *Horses*. New York: Continuum, 2008.

Sicart, Miguel. *Play Matters*. Cambridge, MA: MIT Press, 2014.

Smith, Jonathan Z. *Imagining Religion: From Babylon to Jonestown*. Chicago: University of Chicago Press, 1982.

———. *Map Is Not Territory: Studies in the History of Religions*. Leiden: Brill, 1978.

———. *On Teaching Religion: Essays by Jonathan Z. Smith*. Edited by Christopher I. Lehrich. Oxford: Oxford University Press, 2013.

———. *Relating Religion: Essays in the Study of Religion*. Chicago: University of Chicago Press, 2004.

Smith, Patti. *Horses*. Arista 07822-18827-2, 1996, compact disc. Originally released in 1975.

———. *Patti Smith Complete: 1975–2006; Lyrics, Reflections, and Notes for the Future*. New York: Harper Perennial, 2006.

Smith, Susan Valeria Harris. "Masks in the Modern Drama." PhD diss., Northwestern University, 1979.

Spatz, Ben. *What a Body Can Do: Technique as Knowledge, Practice as Research*. New York: Routledge, 2015.

Spillers, Hortense J. *Black, White, and in Color: Essays on American Literature and Culture*. Chicago: University of Chicago Press, 2003.

Stacy, James R. "The Sun and the Horse: Peter Shaffer's Search for Worship." *Educational Theatre Journal* 28, no. 3 (1976): 325–37.

Stausberg, Michael, and Steven Engler, eds. *The Oxford Handbook of the Study of Religion*. Oxford: Oxford University Press, 2016.

Stucky, Nathan. "Deep Embodiment: The Epistemology of Natural Performance." In *Teaching Performance Studies*, edited by Nathan Stucky and Cynthia Wimmer, 131–44. Carbondale: Southern Illinois University Press, 2002.

Szondi, Peter. *An Essay on the Tragic*. Translated by Paul Fleming. Stanford, CA: Stanford University Press, 2002.

Tambiah, Stanley J. "A Performative Approach to Ritual." *Proceedings of the British Academy* 65 (1979): 113–69.

Taussig, Michael. "Transgression." In Taylor, *Critical Terms for Religious Studies*, 349–64.

Taylor, Diana. "Double-Blind: The Torture Case." *Critical Inquiry* 33, no. 4 (2007): 710–33.

———. *Performance*. Durham, NC: Duke University Press, 2016.

Taylor, Mark C., ed. *Critical Terms for Religious Studies*. Chicago: University of Chicago Press, 1998.

Timm, Neil. "*Equus* as a Modern Tragedy." *Philological Papers* 25 (1979): 128–34.

Tweed, Thomas A. *Religion: A Very Short Introduction*. Oxford: Oxford University Press, 2020.

Walker, Elaine. *Horse*. London: Reaktion Books, 2008.

Walls, Doyle W. "*Equus*: Shaffer, Nietzsche, and the Neuroses of Health." *Modern Drama* 27, no. 3 (1984): 314–23.

Watson, Ariel. "The Anxious Triangle: Modern Metatheatres of the Playwright, Actor, and Spectator." PhD diss., Yale University, 2008.

Watson, John Clair. "The Ritual Plays of Peter Shaffer." PhD diss., University of Oregon, 1987.

Weeks, Jeffrey. *The Languages of Sexuality*. New York: Routledge, 2011.

Woodruff, Paul. *The Necessity of Theatre: The Art of Watching and Being Watched*. Oxford: Oxford University P

INDEX